Better Homes and Gardens®

cherished quilts

for Babies and Kids

FAVORITES FROM THE EDITORS OF AMERICAN PATCHWORK & QUILTING®

From Baby and Kid Projects to High School Graduation Gifts

WILEY

John Wiley & Sons, Inc.

contents

babies

kids

teens

etc.

welcome!

Children of all ages have a way of melting hearts and bringing out our creative side.

Have a new baby in your life? Celebrate by stitching a crib quilt in soft flannel or a personalized wall hanging for the nursery. How about an adventurous toddler? Appliqué an adorable dinosaur quilt for his room. A girly girl? Sew a frilly floral apron. Or perhaps your special kid is a teenager—whip up a keepsake quilt using T-shirts collected from their various activities.

Whomever you are quilting for, this book is brimming with ideas for the quilter looking for heirloom-quality projects for children of all ages. Not only will you enjoy the creative process, but you'll love knowing that your creation will be cherished for years to come.
—Happy Quilting!

babies

When it comes to the littlest ones in our lives, all things soft and cuddly rule. Encourage peaceful naps, contagious giggles, and plenty of snuggle time with these irresistible quilts and accessories.

just *ducky*

Here's a sweet flannel quilt suitable for your favorite little one—boy or girl. The simple appliqué is an updated take on old-fashioned pull toys.

DESIGNER **BONNIE SULLIVAN**   MACHINE QUILTER **BARBARA ANDERSON**
PHOTOGRAPHER **KATHRYN GAMBLE**

materials

- ▸ 2 yards cream-and-blue plaid flannel (blocks, border)
- ▸ ⅜ yard yellow herringbone flannel (duck body and head appliqués)
- ▸ 7" square of gold basket-weave flannel (beak appliqués)
- ▸ 10" square of orange houndstooth flannel (wing appliqués)
- ▸ 9×12" rectangle of dark pink basket-weave flannel (wheel appliqués)
- ▸ 6—9×22" pieces (fat eighths) assorted blue print flannels (blocks, border)
- ▸ ½ yard blue houndstooth flannel (block, border, binding)
- ▸ 2¼ yards backing fabric
- ▸ 51" square batting
- ▸ Cardstock
- ▸ Freezer paper
- ▸ Spray starch
- ▸ 12—¼"-diameter black buttons

Finished quilt: 44½" square   Finished block: 8" square

Quantities are for 44/45"-wide, 100% cotton fabrics. Measurements include ¼" seam allowances. Sew with right sides together unless otherwise stated.

cut fabrics

Cut pieces in the following order. Patterns are on *Pattern Sheet 1.*

   Note: To make easy, perfect circles, use cardstock to cut and prepare the A and E circle appliqués. See Make and Use Templates, *page 154,* to make A and E cardstock templates and cut out fabric circles, being sure to add ³⁄₁₆" seam allowances. Then follow instructions in Prepare Circle Appliqués on *page 10.*

   Bonnie used a freezer-paper-and-starch method to prepare B, C, and D appliqués. To use this technique, see Prepare Remaining Appliqués on *page 10.*

From cream-and-blue plaid flannel, cut:

- 12—8½" squares
- 12—2½×8½" rectangles
- 60—2½×4½" rectangles
- 26—3" squares*

From yellow herringbone flannel, cut:

- 12 of Pattern A
- 6 each of patterns B and B reversed

From gold basket-weave flannel, cut:

- 6 each of patterns C and C reversed

From orange houndstooth flannel, cut:

- 6 each of patterns D and D reversed

From dark pink basket-weave flannel, cut:

- 12 of Pattern E

From each assorted blue print flannel, cut:

- 4—3" squares*
- 11—2½" squares (you will use 64 total)

From blue houndstooth flannel, cut:

- 5—2½×42" binding strips
- 2—3" squares*
- 8—2½" squares

*Because of the thickness of flannel, Bonnie cuts these squares larger than necessary, then trims the finished triangle-squares. If you want to avoid the trimming step, cut 2⅞" squares instead.

prepare circle appliqués

[1] Sew a long basting stitch around edges of a yellow herringbone A circle. Place a cardstock A template on wrong side of fabric circle, then pull up basting stitches to gather fabric snugly around cardstock (Diagram 1). Spray with starch, press, and let dry.

[2] Repeat Step 1 to prepare all 12 yellow herringbone A circles and all 12 dark pink basket-weave E circles.

[3] When you are ready to appliqué the circles, clip gathering threads and gently remove cardstock templates.

prepare remaining appliqués

[1] Lay freezer paper, shiny side down, over patterns B, C, and D. Trace each

DIAGRAM 1   DIAGRAM 2

pattern the number of times indicated in cutting instructions. Cut out freezer-paper shapes on drawn lines.

[2] Using a hot dry iron, press freezer-paper shapes, shiny sides down, onto designated fabrics' wrong sides; let cool. Cut out each shape, adding a generous ¼" seam allowance to all edges.

[3] Spray a small amount of starch into a dish. Place a template-topped appliqué piece on a pressing surface covered with a tea towel or muslin. Dip a cotton swab in starch and moisten seam allowance of appliqué piece (Diagram 2).

[4] Using tip of a hot dry iron, turn seam allowance over edge of freezer-paper template and press until fabric is dry. Press entire seam allowance in the same manner, adding starch as necessary and ensuring fabric is pressed taut against template. Carefully peel off template.

[5] Repeat steps 3 and 4 to prepare all B, C, and D appliqués.

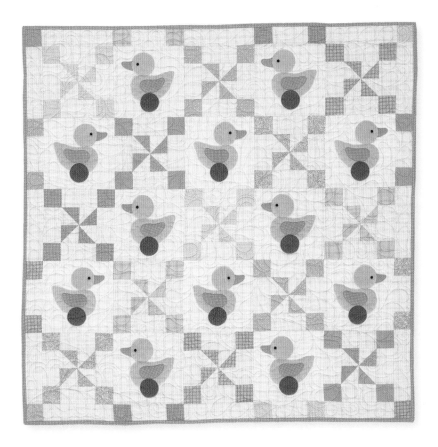

square. Sew together with two seams, stitching ¼" on each side of drawn line (**Diagram 5**). Cut pair apart on drawn line to make two triangle units. Open triangle units and press seams toward blue print to make two triangle-squares. Trim each triangle-square to 2½" square including seam allowances. Repeat to make four matching triangle-squares total.

[**3**] Sew together triangle-squares in pairs (**Diagram 6**). Press seams in opposite directions. Join pairs to make a pinwheel unit. Press seam in one direction. The pinwheel unit should be 4½" square including seam allowances.

assemble appliqué blocks

[**1**] Referring to **Diagram 3**, lay out prepared appliqué pieces on a cream-and-blue plaid 8½" square. Baste in place. Using threads that match the appliqué pieces and a narrow machine zigzag stitch, sew around each piece to make Appliqué Block A. The block should be 8½" square including seam allowances. Repeat to make six total of Appliqué Block A.

[**2**] Using B reversed, C reversed, and D reversed pieces, repeat Step 1 to make six total of Appliqué Block B (**Diagram 4**).

assemble pieced blocks

[**1**] Use a pencil to mark a diagonal line on wrong side of each cream-and-blue plaid 3" square.

[**2**] Layer a marked cream-and-blue plaid 3" square atop an assorted blue print 3"

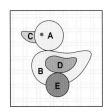

**APPLIQUÉ BLOCK A
DIAGRAM 3**

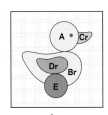

**APPLIQUÉ BLOCK B
DIAGRAM 4**

DIAGRAM 5   **DIAGRAM 6**

[4] Referring to **Diagram 7**, lay out pinwheel unit, four 2½" squares from the same blue print used in triangle-squares, and four cream-and-blue plaid 2½×4½" rectangles in three rows. Sew together pieces in each row. Press seams toward rectangles. Join rows to make a pieced block. Press seams away from center row. The block should be 8½" square including seam allowances.

[5] Using assorted blue print and blue houndstooth 3" and 2½" squares, repeat steps 2–4 to make 13 pieced blocks total (two blocks from each assorted blue print and one block from blue houndstooth).

assemble quilt center

[1] Referring to **Quilt Assembly Diagram**, lay out appliqué and pieced blocks in five rows, alternating appliqué blocks A and B with each row. Sew together blocks in each row. Press seams toward appliqué blocks.

[2] Join rows to make quilt center. Press seams toward rows with A appliqué blocks. The quilt center should be 40½" square including seam allowances.

assemble and add border

[1] Sew together a cream-and-blue plaid 2½×4½" rectangle and two matching blue print 2½" squares to make a border unit (**Diagram 8**). Press seams toward rectangle. The border unit should be 2½×8½" including seam allowances. Using assorted blue print and blue houndstooth 2½" squares, repeat to make eight border units total (one unit from each assorted blue print and two units from blue houndstooth).

[2] Referring to **Quilt Assembly Diagram**, sew together two border units and three cream-and-blue plaid 2½×8½" rectangles to make a border strip. Press seams toward rectangles. The border strip should be 2½×40½" including seam allowances. Repeat to make four border strips total.

[3] Sew border strips to opposite edges of quilt center. Press seams toward border.

tip

Instead of sewing buttons on a baby quilt, consider the following alternatives to make ¼"-diameter black circles for the duck eyes: fusible-appliqué, a machine or hand satin stitch, or a fine-point permanent fabric marker.

[4] Join assorted blue print 2½" squares to ends of remaining border strips. Press seams toward border strips. Add border strips to remaining edges of quilt center to complete quilt top. Press seams toward border.

finish quilt

[1] Layer quilt top, batting, and backing; baste. (For details, see Complete the Quilt, *page 158.*)

[2] Quilt as desired. Using yellow thread, Barbara Anderson machine-quilted around the ducks' bodies and wings. She stitched feather designs in the pieced blocks and appliqué backgrounds (**Quilting Diagram**).

[3] Using black thread, hand-sew a button on each duck head for an eye. (If the quilt is intended for a baby or small child, see the tip on *page 12* for ideas on what to use instead of the buttons, which can present a choking hazard.)

[4] Bind with blue houndstooth binding strips. (For details, see Better Binding, *page 159.*)

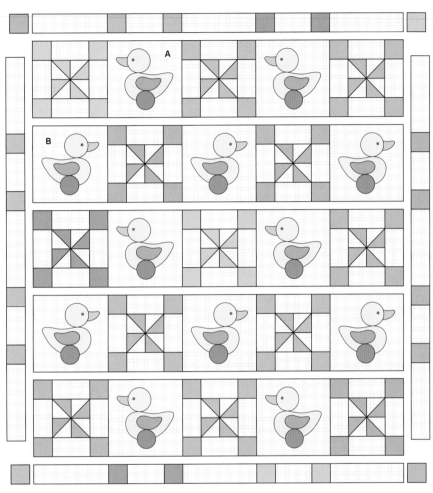

QUILT ASSEMBLY DIAGRAM

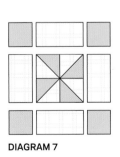

DIAGRAM 7

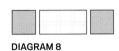

DIAGRAM 8

QUILTING DIAGRAM

baby talk

Polka dot, star, and toile flannels combine for a snuggly crib quilt. You can vary the kaleidoscope design depending on where you place your lights and darks.

DESIGNER **RHODA NELSON**   PHOTOGRAPHER **ADAM ALBRIGHT**

pink-and-brown quilt

materials

- ¾ yard solid cream flannel (blocks)
- ⅔ yard brown small polka dot flannel (blocks, inner border)
- ¾ yard white large polka dot flannel (blocks)
- ⅜ yard pink star print flannel (blocks)
- 1¼ yards pink-and-brown toile flannel (outer border, binding)
- 3 yards backing fabric
- 54" square batting

Finished quilt: 47½" square   Finished block: 12" square

Quantities are for 44/45"-wide, 100% cotton fabrics. Measurements include ¼" seam allowances. Sew with right sides together unless otherwise stated.

cut fabrics

Cut pieces in the following order.

The patterns are on *Pattern Sheet 1.* To make templates of patterns and use them for cutting out pieces, see Make and Use Templates, *page 154.* Be sure to transfer dots to templates, then to fabric pieces. These dots are matching points and are necessary when joining pieces.

From solid cream flannel, cut:
- 36 each of patterns A and C

From brown small polka dot flannel, cut:
- 2—2×39½" inner border strips
- 2—2×36½" inner border strips
- 36 of Pattern B

DIAGRAM 1   **DIAGRAM 2**   **DIAGRAM 3**   **DIAGRAM 4**

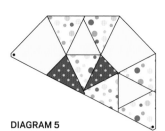

DIAGRAM 5

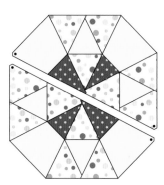

DIAGRAM 6

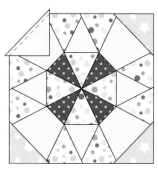

DIAGRAM 7

From white large polka dot flannel, cut:
- 108 of Pattern C

From pink star print flannel, cut:
- 18—3⅞" squares, cutting each in half diagonally for 36 triangles total

From pink-and-brown toile flannel, cut:
- 5—4½×42" strips for outer border
- 5—2½×42" binding strips

assemble blocks

When joining pieces A, B, and C, be sure to align matching points marked on pieces. To do this, push a pin through center of dots on layered pieces.

[1] Referring to **Diagram 1**, sew together a solid cream A piece and a brown small polka dot B triangle to make a narrow pieced triangle. Press seam toward brown polka dot. Repeat to make 36 narrow pieced triangles total.

[2] Aligning marked matching points, sew white large polka dot C triangles to opposite long edges of a solid cream C triangle (**Diagram 2**).

Press seams toward white polka dot triangles.

[3] Add a third white large polka dot C triangle to remaining edge of Step 2 solid cream C triangle to make a wide pieced triangle (**Diagram 3**). Press seam toward solid cream triangle.

[4] Repeat steps 2 and 3 to make 36 wide pieced triangles total.

[5] Sew together a narrow pieced triangle and a wide pieced triangle to make a triangle pair (**Diagram 4**). Press seam toward wide pieced triangle. Repeat to make 36 triangle pairs total.

[6] Sew together two triangle pairs to make a half unit (**Diagram 5**). Press seam toward wide pieced triangle. Repeat with remaining pairs to make 18 half units total.

[7] Join two half units to make a center unit (**Diagram 6**). Press seam in one direction. Repeat to make nine center units total.

[8] Add a pink star print triangle to a corner of a center unit; press seam toward pink star print. Repeat with remaining corners of center unit to make a block (**Diagram 7**). The block should be 12½"

square including seam allowances. Repeat to make nine blocks total.

assemble quilt center

[1] Referring to **Quilt Assembly Diagram**, sew together blocks in three rows. Press seams in one direction, alternating direction with each row.

[2] Join rows to make quilt center. Press seams in one direction. The quilt center should be 36½" square including seam allowances.

add border

[1] Sew short brown small polka dot inner border strips to opposite edges of quilt center. Add long brown small polka dot inner border strips to remaining edges. Press all seams toward border.

[2] Cut and piece pink-and-brown toile 4½×42" strips to make:
  ‣ 2—4½×47½" outer border strips
  ‣ 2—4½×39½" outer border strips

[3] Sew short outer border strips to opposite edges of quilt center. Add long outer border strips to remaining edges to complete quilt top. Press all seams toward outer border.

finish quilt

[1] Layer backing, batting, and quilt top; baste. (For details, see Complete the Quilt, *page 158*.)

[2] Quilt as desired. The featured quilt is machine-quilted with an allover swirl design in the quilt center and inner border and a meandering ivy design in the outer border (**Quilting Diagram**).

QUILTING DIAGRAM

[3] Bind with pink-and-brown toile binding strips. (For details, see Better Binding, *page 159*.)

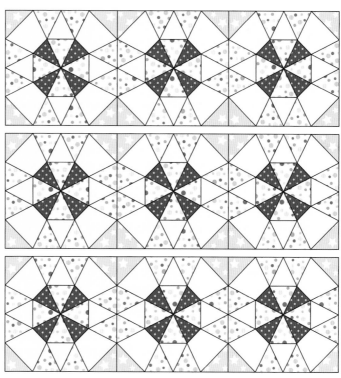

QUILT ASSEMBLY DIAGRAM

blue-and-brown quilt

materials

- ½ yard solid cream flannel (blocks)
- ⅔ blue star print flannel (blocks)
- ¾ yard white large polka dot flannel (blocks)
- ⅝ yard brown small polka dot flannel (blocks, inner border)
- 1¼ yards blue-and-brown toile flannel (outer border, binding)
- 3 yards backing fabric
- 54" square batting

Finished quilt: 47½" square   Finished block: 12" square

Quantities are for 44/45"-wide, 100% cotton fabrics. Measurements include ¼" seam allowances. Sew with right sides together unless otherwise stated.

cut fabrics

Cut pieces in the following order. Patterns are on *Pattern Sheet 1*. To make templates of patterns and use them for cutting out pieces, see Make and Use Templates, *page 154*. Be sure to transfer dots to templates, then to fabric pieces. These dots are matching points and are necessary when joining pieces.

From solid cream flannel, cut:
- 36 of Pattern A

From blue star print flannel, cut:
- 18—3⅞" squares, cutting each in half diagonally for 36 triangles total
- 36 of Pattern B

From white large polka dot flannel, cut:
- 108 of Pattern C

From brown small polka dot flannel, cut:
- 2—2×39½" inner border strips
- 2—2×36½" inner border strips
- 36 of Pattern C

From blue-and-brown toile flannel, cut:
- 5—4½×42" strips for outer border
- 5—2½×42" binding strips

assemble blocks

[1] Referring to Pink-and-Brown Quilt, Assemble Blocks, Step 1 (*page 16*), use solid cream A pieces and blue star print B triangles to make 36 narrow pieced triangles.

[2] Referring to Pink-and-Brown Quilt, Assemble Blocks, Steps 2 and 3, use white large polka dot C triangles and brown small polka dot C triangles to make 36 wide pieced triangles.

[3] Referring to Pink-and-Brown Quilt, Assemble Blocks, steps 5–7, make nine center units.

[**4**] Referring to Pink-and-Brown Quilt, Assemble Blocks, Step 8, add blue star print triangles to center units to make nine blocks (**Diagram 8**).

assemble quilt center

[**1**] Referring to **Quilt Assembly Diagram**, sew together blocks in three rows. Press seams in one direction, alternating direction with each row.

[**2**] Join rows to make quilt center. Press seams in one direction. The quilt center should be 36½" square including seam allowances.

add border

[**1**] Sew short brown small polka dot inner border strips to opposite edges of quilt center. Add long brown small polka dot inner border strips to remaining edges. Press all seams toward border.

[**2**] Cut and piece blue-and-brown toile 4½×42" strips to make:
▸ 2—4½×47½" outer border strips
▸ 2—4½×39½" outer border strips

[**3**] Sew short outer border strips to opposite edges of quilt center. Add long outer border strips to remaining edges to complete quilt top. Press all seams toward outer border.

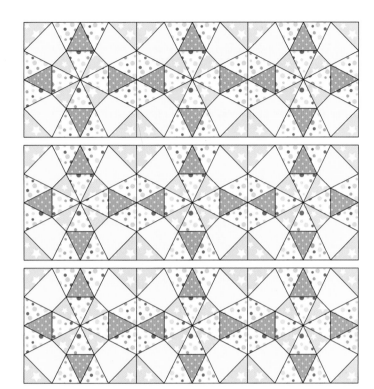

QUILT ASSEMBLY DIAGRAM

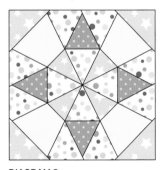

DIAGRAM 8

QUILTING DIAGRAM

finish quilt

[**1**] Layer backing, batting, and quilt top; baste. (For details, see Complete the Quilt, *page 158*.)

[**2**] Quilt as desired. The featured quilt is stitched with an allover swirl design in the quilt center and inner border and a loop-and-star design in the outer border (**Quilting Diagram**).

[**3**] Bind with blue-and-brown toile binding strips. (For details, see Better Binding, *page 159*.)

around the block

Dazzle a toddler or a newborn with a smorgasbord of cheerful polka-dot fabrics splashed across an oversize Log Cabin block.

DESIGNER **JENNIFER KELTNER**   MACHINE QUILTER **NANCY SHARR**
PHOTOGRAPHER **ADAM ALBRIGHT**

materials

- 3½ yards total assorted polka dots in cream, blue, yellow, green, and red (block)
- ½ yard black-and-cream polka dot (binding)
- 3¼ yards backing fabric (see fabric notes below)
- 58" square batting

Finished baby quilt: 51½" square

Quantities are for 44/45"-wide fabrics.
Measurements include ¼" seam allowances. Sew with right sides together unless otherwise stated.

fabric notes

Bright polka dots of all sizes and colors make this quilt a hit with little ones. The common link among the fabrics is the cream background or polka dots.

For an oh-so-soft quilt, use plush fabric for the backing. Most cuddly fleece fabric is 59" wide so you'll need just 1⅔ yards for the backing.

cut fabrics

Cut pieces in the following order.

From assorted polka dots, cut:
- 2—6½×42" strips, cutting and piecing them to make one 6½×51½" rectangle for Position 16
- 2—7½×42" strips, cutting and piecing them to make one 7½×45½" rectangle for Position 15
- 2—6½×42" strips, cutting and piecing them to make one 6½×44½" rectangle for Position 14
- 1—6½×39½" rectangle for Position 13
- 1—8×38½" rectangle for Position 12

- 1—8×32" rectangle for Position 11
- 1—6½×31" rectangle for Position 10
- 1—6×26" rectangle for Position 9
- 1—5×25½" rectangle for Position 8
- 1—5×21½" rectangle for Position 7
- 1—6½×21" rectangle for Position 6
- 1—7×15½" rectangle for Position 5
- 1—6×14½" rectangle for Position 4
- 1—5×10" rectangle for Position 3
- 1—4½×10" rectangle for Position 2
- 1—3½×6" rectangle for Position 1
- 1—6×7" rectangle for block center

From black-and-cream polka dot, cut:

- 6—2½×42" binding strips

assemble quilt top

[1] Sew assorted polka dot Position 1 rectangle to top edge of assorted polka dot 6×7" block center (**Diagram 1**). Press seam away from block center.

[2] Add assorted polka dot Position 2 rectangle to left-hand edge of Step 1 unit (**Diagram 2**). Press seam as before.

DIAGRAM 1

DIAGRAM 2

DIAGRAM 3

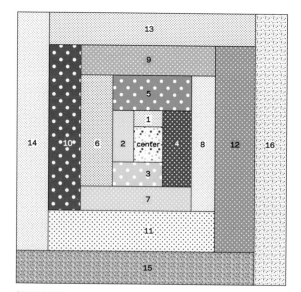

QUILT ASSEMBLY DIAGRAM

[3] Add assorted polka dot Position 3 rectangle to bottom edge of Step 2 unit; press as before (Diagram 3).

[4] Referring to **Quilt Assembly Diagram**, continue sewing rectangles in a counterclockwise direction to make a Log Cabin block. Press all seams away from block center. The block, or quilt top, should be 51 ½" square including seam allowances.

finish quilt

[1] Layer quilt top, batting, and backing; baste. (For details, see Complete the Quilt, *page 158*.)

[2] Quilt as desired. This quilt features a looped meandering design across the quilt top to continue the polka dot theme.

tips for backing a quilt with minkee* or other plush fabric

‣ Minkee is the name Benartex gives to the soft, knit-back fleece they produce. (Dot red Minkee Blankee is shown *below right*.)
‣ Minkee stretches crosswise but very little along the lengthwise grain (parallel to the selvages).
‣ After cutting a plush fabric such as Minkee, machine-dry the piece for a few minutes to remove the "fluffies" or "pills."
‣ Use a lightweight, low-loft batting.
‣ Baste the quilt sandwich or pin liberally to keep layers together. Begin at center and work out toward the quilt edges.
‣ Use a new needle. For straight-line quilting, set the stitch length to about eight stitches per inch.
‣ Use a walking foot to prevent the fabric from slipping as you sew straight lines.
‣ Clean the throat plate, feed dogs, and bobbin case often.

[3] Bind with black-and-cream polka dot binding strips. (For details, see Better Binding, *page 159*.)

color option

Need a great graduation gift? Look for a common color theme among a graduate's prized T-shirts and use that as a guide for selecting fabrics for this black-and-white version of "Around the Block." It will pay tribute to the graduate's achievements and provide a great wrap-up and cozy remembrance of home.

optical illusion

This nursery stunner may look like it's intricately pieced,
but it's actually fast-and-easy appliqué on a classic Snowball block.

DESIGNER **ALLISON JANE SMITH**   PHOTOGRAPHER **GREG SCHEIDEMANN**

materials

- 20—18×22" pieces (fat quarters) assorted prints and stripes in yellow, pink, blue, green, and brown (blocks, appliqués, border)
- ½ yard brown-and-pink print (binding)
- 3 yards backing fabric
- 56" square batting
- Lightweight fusible web
- Monofilament thread

Finished quilt: 49½" square   Finished block: 9" square

Quantities are for 44/45"-wide, 100% cotton fabrics. Measurements include ¼" seam allowances. Sew with right sides together unless otherwise stated.

cut fabrics

Cut pieces in the following order. Patterns are on *Pattern Sheet 1*. To use fusible web for appliquéing, complete the following steps.

[1] Lay fusible web, paper side up, over patterns. Use a pencil to trace each pattern the number of times indicated in cutting instructions, leaving ½" between tracings. Cut out fusible-web shapes roughly ¼" outside traced lines.

[2] Following manufacturer's instructions, press each fusible-web shape onto wrong side of designated fabric; let cool. Cut out fabric shapes on drawn lines; peel off paper backings.

From assorted fat quarters, cut:

- 25—9½" squares
- 20—2½×9½" rectangles
- 100—2½" squares (25 sets of 4 matching squares for blocks)
- 40—2½" squares (20 sets of 2 matching squares for border units)
- 8—2½" squares for triangle-squares
- 25 of Pattern A

- ▸ 100 of Pattern B (25 sets of 4 pieces to match each Pattern A piece)
- ▸ 100 of Pattern C (25 sets of 4 matching pieces)

From brown-and-pink print, cut:
- ▸ 5—2½×42" binding strips

assemble blocks

[1] Use a pencil to mark a diagonal line on wrong side of each 2½" square. (To prevent fabric from stretching as you draw the lines, place 220-grit sandpaper under squares.)

[2] Align a marked square with one corner of an assorted print 9½" square (**Diagram 1**; note direction of marked line). Sew on drawn line; trim excess fabric, leaving ¼" seam allowance. Press open attached triangle.

[3] Repeat Step 2 to add three matching marked squares to remaining corners of 9½" square to make a Snowball block (**Diagram 1**; again note direction of drawn lines). The block should be 9½" square including seam allowances.

[4] Repeat steps 2 and 3 to make 25 Snowball blocks total.

appliqué blocks

Referring to **Appliqué Placement Diagram**, lay out appliqué pieces on one block; fuse in place. Using monofilament thread or threads that match the appliqués, straight-stitch or zigzag-stitch close to edges of each appliqué piece. Repeat to appliqué each block.

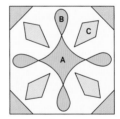

APPLIQUÉ PLACEMENT DIAGRAM

tip

Create placement guidelines on each block to help you arrange appliqué shapes evenly. Fold the blocks in half vertically and horizontally and finger-press. Then fold in both directions diagonally and finger-press.

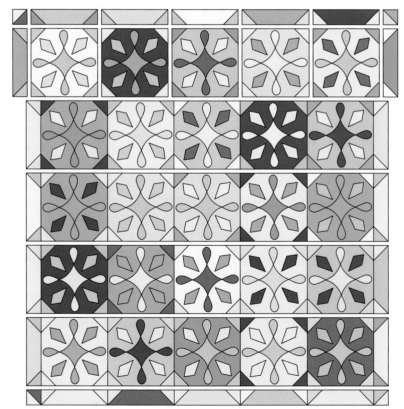

QUILT ASSEMBLY DIAGRAM

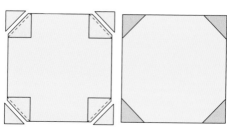

DIAGRAM 1

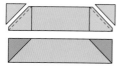

DIAGRAM 2

DIAGRAM 3

assemble border units

[1] Align a marked 2½" square on one end of an assorted print 2½×9½" rectangle (**Diagram 2**; note direction of marked line). Sew on marked line; trim excess fabric, leaving ¼" seam allowance. Press open attached triangle. Add a matching marked square to opposite end of rectangle to make a border unit (**Diagram 2**; again note direction of marked line). The border unit should still be 2½×9½" including seam allowances. Repeat to make 20 border units total.

[2] Layer two remaining marked 2½" squares, aligning lines. Sew together on one marked line; trim excess fabric, leaving ¼" seam allowance (**Diagram 3**). Press unit open to make a triangle-square. The triangle-square should be 2½" square including seam allowances. Repeat to make four triangle-squares total.

assemble quilt top

[1] Referring to **Quilt Assembly Diagram**, lay out blocks, border units, and triangle-squares in seven horizontal rows.

[2] Sew together pieces in each row. Press seams in one direction, alternating direction with each row.

[3] Join rows to complete quilt top. Press seams in one direction.

finish quilt

[1] Layer quilt top, batting, and backing; baste. (For details, see Complete the Quilt, *page 158*.)

[2] Quilt as desired. This quilt features a swirl-and-leaf design stitched across the quilt top.

[3] Bind with brown-and-pink print binding strips. (For details, see Better Binding, *page 159*.)

story *time*

Soft chenille and peppy, polka dot pinwheels
make this vintage-inspired design the perfect gift
to celebrate a new baby's birth.

DESIGNER **KATIE HENNAGIR**   MACHINE QUILTER **JACE HENNAGIR**
PHOTOGRAPHER **GREG SCHEIDEMANN**

materials

- ▸ 2 yards cream-and-blue plaid flannel (blocks, border)
- ▸ ⅞ yard each of turquoise, red, and yellow polka dots (blocks)
- ▸ ¼ yard each of red, turquoise, and yellow chenilles (setting squares)
- ▸ 1⅛ yards multicolor stripe (inner border, binding)
- ▸ ⅞ yard yellow print (outer border)
- ▸ 3 yards backing fabric
- ▸ 54×61" batting

Finished quilt: 47½×54½"   Finished block: 7" square

Quantities are for 44/45"-wide, 100% cotton fabrics.
Measurements include ¼" seam allowances. Sew with
right sides together unless otherwise stated.

cut fabrics

Cut the pieces in the following order.

From each red, turquoise, and yellow polka dot, cut:
- ▸ 60—4" squares

From each red, turquoise, and yellow chenille, cut:
- ▸ 5—7½" squares

From multicolor stripe, cut:
- ▸ 5—2×42" strips for inner border
- ▸ 1—27" square, cutting it into enough 2½"-wide bias strips to total 220" for binding (For details, see Cutting Bias Strips, *page 158*.)

From yellow print, cut:
- ▸ 5—5×42" strips for outer border

assemble
pinwheel blocks

[1] Use a quilter's pencil to mark a diagonal line on wrong side of turquoise polka dot 4" squares.

[2] Layer a marked turquoise polka dot 4" square atop a red polka dot 4" square.

Sew on the drawn line; trim excess, leaving ¼" seam allowance (**Diagram 1**). Press seam toward red polka dot to make a triangle-square. Repeat to make 60 triangle-squares total.

[3] Mark a diagonal line on wrong side of yellow polka dot 4" squares.

[4] Layer a marked yellow polka dot 4" square atop a triangle-square (**Diagram 2**; note direction of drawn line and position of turquoise polka dot). Sew on drawn line; trim excess, leaving ¼" seam allowance, to make a triangle unit. Press seam toward yellow polka dot. The triangle unit should be 4" square including seam allowances. Repeat to make 60 triangle units total.

[5] Sew together triangle units in pairs (**Diagram 3**). Press seams toward red polka dot. Join pairs to make a Pinwheel block. Press seam open to reduce bulk. The Pinwheel block should be 7½" square including seam allowances. Repeat to make 15 Pinwheel blocks total.

assemble
quilt center

[1] Referring to **Quilt Assembly Diagram**, lay out Pinwheel blocks and red, turquoise, and yellow chenille 7½" setting squares in six rows.

[2] Sew together pieces in each row. Press seams in one direction, alternating direction with each row.

[3] Join rows to make quilt center. Press seams in one direction. The quilt center should be 35½×42½" including seam allowances.

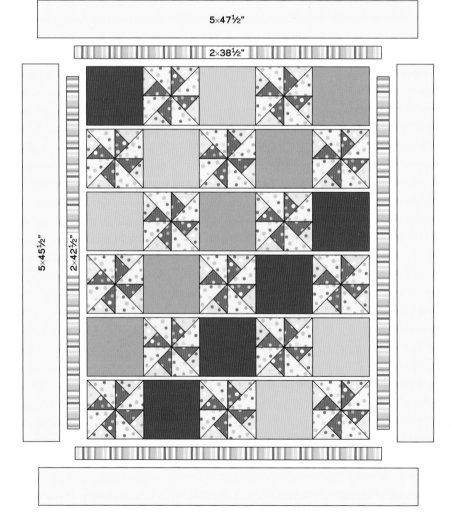

5×47½"

2×38½"

5×45½"

2×42½"

QUILT ASSEMBLY DIAGRAM

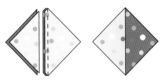

DIAGRAM 1

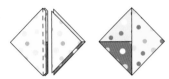

DIAGRAM 2

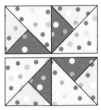

DIAGRAM 3

assemble and add borders

[1] Cut and piece multicolor stripe 2×42" strips to make:
  ▸ 2—2×42½" inner border strips
  ▸ 2—2×38½" inner border strips

[2] Sew long inner border strips to side edges of quilt center. Add short inner border strips to remaining edges. Press all seams toward border.

[3] Cut and piece yellow print 5×42" strips to make:
  ▸ 2—5×47½" outer border strips
  ▸ 2—5×45½" outer border strips

[4] Sew short outer border strips to side edges of quilt center. Add long outer border strips to remaining edges to complete quilt top. Press all seams toward outer border.

finish quilt

[1] Layer quilt top, batting, and backing; baste. (For details, see Complete the Quilt, *page 158*.)

[2] Quilt as desired. This quilt features a meandering design of loops and swirls stitched across the quilt top.

[3] Bind with multicolor stripe bias binding strips. (For details, see Better Binding, *page 159*.)

B is for *baby*

Classic monogrammed crib quilts in timeless color schemes are perfect for every baby—girl or boy.

DESIGNERS **CORI DERKSEN AND MYRA HARDER**
PHOTOGRAPHERS **GREG SCHEIDEMANN AND JAY WILDE**

baby girl quilt

materials

- ▸ 1⅛ yards ivory print (sashing, binding, and border)
- ▸ 18×22" piece (fat quarter) pink tone-on-tone print (appliqué foundation)
- ▸ ½ yard each of two assorted pink prints (quilt center)
- ▸ ¼ yard each of two assorted pink prints (quilt center)
- ▸ 18×22" piece (fat quarter) dark pink tone-on-tone print (monogram appliqué)
- ▸ 1⅜ yards backing fabric
- ▸ 42×49" batting

Finished quilt: 35½×42½"

Quantities are for 44/45"-wide, 100% cotton fabrics. Measurements include ¼" seam allowances. Sew with right sides together unless otherwise stated.

cut fabrics

Cut pieces in the following order. The appliqué patterns are on *Pattern Sheet 1*. To make pattern templates, see Make and Use Templates, *page 154*. Add ³⁄₁₆" seam allowances when cutting out the appliqué pieces.

From ivory print, cut:

- ▸ 4—2½×42" binding strips
- ▸ 2—3½×36½" border strips
- ▸ 2—3½×35½" border strips
- ▸ 2—2½×14½" rectangles
- ▸ 2—2½×8½" rectangles
- ▸ 1—1½×18½" sashing strip
- ▸ 2—1½×8" sashing strips
- ▸ 1—1½×6½" sashing strip

From pink tone-on-tone print, cut:
- 1—8½×10½" appliqué foundation

From each ½-yard pink print, cut:
- 1—14½×18½" rectangle
- 1—8×6" rectangle

From each ¼-yard pink print, cut:
- 1—14½×6½" rectangle
- 1—8×6" rectangle

From dark pink tone-on-tone print, cut:
- 1 each of patterns A and B

assemble quilt center

[1] Sew ivory print 2½×8½" rectangles to opposite short edges of the pink tone-on-tone print appliqué foundation (**Block Assembly Diagram**). Sew ivory print 2½×14½" rectangles to remaining edges to make a center block. The center

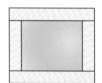

BLOCK ASSEMBLY DIAGRAM

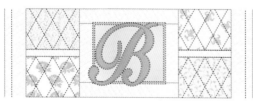

QUILTING DIAGRAM

block should be 14½×12½" including seam allowances. Press all seams toward the ivory print.

[2] Lay out the center block, pink print rectangles, and ivory print sashing strips (**Quilt Assembly Diagram**). Join the pieces in sections and the sections in rows. Join the rows to make the quilt center. Press all seams toward the pink prints. The quilt center should be 29½×36½" including seam allowances.

add border and appliqué monogram

[1] Sew ivory print 3½×36½" border strips to quilt center's long edges. Sew ivory print 3½×35½" border strips to remaining edges to complete the quilt top. Press all seams toward border.

[2] Referring to photo at right, position appliqué pieces A and B on the center block; baste. Working from the bottom layer to the top, needle-turn appliqué the pieces in place.

finish quilt

[1] Layer quilt top, batting, and backing. (For details, see Complete the Quilt on *page 158.*)

[2] Quilt as desired. This quilt was machine-quilted with a 60° diamond grid over the quilt center (**Quilting Diagram**), leaving the

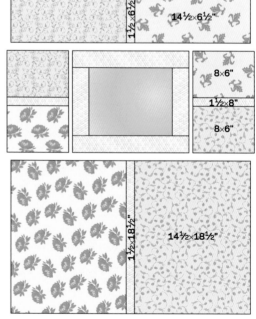

QUILT ASSEMBLY DIAGRAM

tip

Want to personalize your quilt by monogramming the baby's first initial in place of the B? Simply find a font you like on your computer, then enlarge it to the desired size to make your own monogram pattern.

appliqué foundation, monogram, sashing, and border unstitched. The monogram and the appliqué foundation center were outline quilted and stitched in the ditch on the sashing. A straight line was stitched about 1¼" from the outer edge of the border.

[3] Use ivory print binding strips to bind quilt. (For details, see Better Binding, *page 159.*)

baby boy quilt

materials

- 1 ⅓ yards blue tone-on-tone print (sashing, monogram appliqué, binding, and border)
- 1—18×22" piece (fat quarter) green tone-on-tone print (appliqué foundation)
- ½ yard blue print (quilt center)
- ½ yard green print (quilt center)
- 1⅜ yards backing fabric
- 42×49" batting

Finished quilt: 35½×42½"

Quantities are for 44/45"-wide, 100% cotton fabrics.
Measurements include ¼" seam allowances. Sew with right sides together unless otherwise stated.

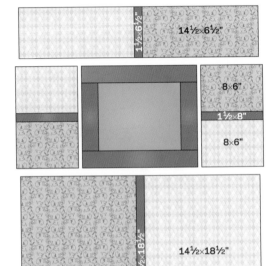

QUILT ASSEMBLY DIAGRAM

cut fabrics

Cut pieces in the following order. The appliqué patterns are on *Pattern Sheet 1*. To make pattern templates, see Make and Use Templates, *page 154*. Add ³⁄₁₆" seam allowances when cutting out appliqué pieces.

From blue tone-on-tone print, cut:
- 4—2½×42" binding strips
- 2—3½×36½" border strips
- 2—3½×35½" border strips
- 2—2½×14½" rectangles
- 2—2½×8½" rectangles
- 1—1½×18½" sashing strip
- 2—1½×8" sashing strips
- 1—1½×6½" sashing strip
- 1 each of patterns A and B

From green tone-on-tone print, cut:
- 1—8½×10½" appliqué foundation

From blue print, cut:
- 1—14½×18½" rectangle
- 1—14½×6½" rectangle
- 2—8×6" rectangles

From green print, cut:
- 1—14½×18½" rectangle
- 1—14½×6½" rectangle
- 2—8×6" rectangles

BLOCK ASSEMBLY DIAGRAM

QUILTING DIAGRAM

assemble quilt center

[1] Sew blue tone-on-tone print 2½×8½" rectangles to opposite short edges of the green tone-on-tone print 8½×10½" appliqué foundation (**Block Assembly Diagram**). Sew blue tone-on-tone print 2½×14½" rectangles to remaining edges to make a center block. The center block should be 14½×12½" including seam allowances. Press all seams toward blue tone-on-tone print.

[2] Lay out the center block, blue print and green print rectangles, and blue tone-on-tone print sashing strips (**Quilt Assembly Diagram**). Join the pieces in sections and the sections in rows. Press all seams toward the sashing strips. Join the rows to make the quilt center. Press seams in one direction. The quilt center should be 29½×36½" including seam allowances.

add border and appliqué monogram

[1] Sew the blue tone-on-tone print 3½×36½" border strips to quilt center's long edges. Sew blue tone-on-tone print 3½×35½" border strips to remaining edges to complete the quilt top. Press all seams toward border.

[2] Referring to photo above, position appliqué pieces A and B on the center block; baste. Working from the bottom layer to the top, needle-turn appliqué the pieces in place.

finish quilt

[1] Layer quilt top, batting, and backing. (For details, see Complete the Quilt on *page 158*.)

[2] Quilt as desired. This quilt was machine-quilted with horizontal lines about 1½" apart over the quilt center (**Quilting Diagram**), leaving the appliqué foundation, monogram, sashing, and border unstitched. The monogram, appliqué foundation center, and sashing were stitched in the ditch. Two straight lines were stitched about 1¼" and 1½" from the outer edges of the border.

[3] Use blue tone-on-tone print binding strips to bind quilt. (For details, see Better Binding, *page 159*.)

monkey see, monkey *duo*

No doubt about it—these colorful bibs are certain to elicit smiles from both toddlers and grown-ups alike.

DESIGNER **LINDA LUM DEBONO**   PHOTOGRAPHER **ADAM ALBRIGHT**

materials for feed me bib

- ▸ 10" square red-orange tone-on-tone (letter appliqués)
- ▸ 2—18×22" pieces (fat quarters) yellow floral (appliqué foundation, bib back)
- ▸ 11×16" batting
- ▸ 10" square lightweight fusible web
- ▸ Thread: red-orange
- ▸ ⅞" square hook-and-loop tape

Finished bib: 9½×13½"

Quantities are for 100% cotton fabrics.
Measurements include ¼" seam allowances. Sew with right sides together unless otherwise stated.

cut fabrics for feed me bib

Cut pieces in the following order. Patterns are on *Pattern Sheet 2*. (For more information on appliqué, see Piece and Appliqué, *page 155*.)

To use fusible web for appliquéing, complete the following steps.

[1] Lay fusible web, paper side up, over patterns. Use a pencil to trace each pattern, leaving ½" between tracings. Cut out fusible-web shapes roughly ¼" outside traced lines.

[2] Following manufacturer's instructions, press fusible-web shapes onto wrong sides of designated fabrics; let cool. Cut out fabric shapes on drawn lines. Peel off paper backings.

From red-orange tone-on-tone, cut:
▸ 1 each of letters F, D, and M
▸ 3 of letter E
▸ 1 of exclamation point

tip

Use tear-away or water-soluble stabilizer beneath appliqué foundation to add support and eliminate puckers and pulling on the fabric as you machine-appliqué. Or you may use freezer paper as a stabilizer.

From yellow floral, cut:
▸ 1 each of patterns A and A reversed

From batting, cut:
▸ 1 of Pattern A

appliqué feed me bib top

[1] Referring to photo *left*, arrange red-orange tone-on-tone letters F, E, E, D, M, E, and exclamation point on yellow floral A foundation. Fuse in place.

[2] Using red-orange thread and a short stitch length, machine-zigzag-stitch around each appliqué piece to make bib top.

finish feed me bib

[1] Layer appliquéd bib top atop yellow floral A reverse piece, right sides together. Place on top of batting. Using a ¼" seam, sew around edges, leaving a 3" opening along one side for turning. Clip curves and turn bib right side out through opening. Press flat and hand-stitch opening closed.

[2] Sew hook-and-loop tape parts at marks indicated on Pattern A. Straight-stitch around outside edges of tape, using thread to match top and back fabrics, to complete bib.

materials for monkey bib

▸ 18×22" piece (fat quarter) brown tone-on-tone (appliqué, bib back)
▸ 7" square solid tan (appliqués)
▸ 3" square each solid white and solid black (appliqués)
▸ 18×22" piece (fat quarter) green stripe (appliqué foundation)
▸ 11×16" batting
▸ 10" square lightweight fusible web
▸ Thread: brown, black, white
▸ ⅞" square hook-and-loop tape

Finished bib: 9½×13½"

Quantities are for 100% cotton fabrics. Measurements include ¼" seam allowances. Sew with right sides together unless otherwise stated.

cut fabrics
for monkey bib

From brown tone-on-tone, cut:
▸ 1 each of patterns A reversed and B

From solid tan, cut:
▸ 1 each of patterns C, H, I, and J

From solid white, cut:
▸ 1 each of patterns D and E

From solid black, cut:
▸ 1 each of patterns F and G

From green stripe, cut:
▸ 1 of Pattern A

From batting, cut:
▸ 1 of Pattern A

appliqué
monkey bib top

[1] Using a light box or window and a water-soluble pen, mark smile lines on solid tan J piece.

[2] Referring to **Appliqué Placement Diagram**, arrange appliqué pieces B–J on green

stripe A foundation. Fuse in place.

[3] Working from bottom layer toward the top, use brown thread and a short stitch length to machine-zigzag-stitch around edges of pieces B, C, H, I, and J. Use black thread to appliqué edges of pieces D, E, F, and G.

[4] Referring to the photo, *above*, use white thread and a short stitch length to machine-zigzag-stitch dots in appliqué pieces F and G. Use black thread and a short stitch length to machine-zigzag-stitch a smile line (as marked) to make bib top.

finish monkey bib

Referring to Finish Feed Me Bib, steps 1 and 2, use appliquéd bib top, brown tone-on-tone A reverse piece, batting, and hook-and-loop tape to complete bib.

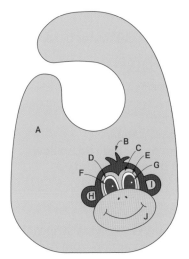

APPLIQUÉ PLACEMENT DIAGRAM

oh, boy!

Forget feminine or floral—this baby quilt uses a variety of fat eighths in primary colors to welcome a little bundle of joy.

QUILTMAKER AND MACHINE QUILTER **STEPHANIE CORINA GODDARD**
PHOTOGRAPHER **CAMERON SADEGHPOUR**

materials

- 1⅓ yards solid white (borders)
- 14—9×22" pieces (fat eighths) assorted red, yellow, and blue prints (blocks, middle border, binding)
- 18×22" piece (fat quarter) multicolor large dot (blocks)
- 9×22" piece (fat eighth) multicolor small dot (blocks)
- 2⅞ yards backing fabric
- 50" square batting

Finished quilt: 44" square   Finished block: 4" square

Quantities are for 44/45"-wide, 100% cotton fabrics. Measurements include ¼" seam allowances. Sew with right sides together unless otherwise stated.

cut fabrics

Cut pieces in the following order. Cut outer and inner borders lengthwise (parallel to the selvage).

From solid white, cut:
- 2—3½×44" outer border strips
- 2—3½×38" outer border strips
- 2—1¾×35" inner border strips
- 2—1¾×32½" inner border strips
- 48—2" squares

From assorted red, yellow, and blue prints, cut:
- 13—2×21" strips
- 29—1¾×21" strips
- 48—2" squares
- Enough 2½"-wide strips in lengths varying from 4½" to 6½" to total 200" for binding

From multicolor large dot, cut:
- 2—2×21" strips
- 2—1¾×21" strips

From multicolor small dot, cut:
- 1—2×21" strip
- 1—1¾×21" strip

assemble blocks

[1] Referring to **Strip Set Diagram**, join two assorted print 1¾×21" strips and an assorted print 2×21" strip to make a strip set. Press seams toward outer strips. Repeat with remaining assorted print strips and multicolor large and small dot strips to make 16 strip sets total.

[2] Cut strip sets into 4½"-wide segments to make 64 Rail Fence blocks total.

tip

Is your quilt center distorted? Try alternating stitching directions when you join rows. Stitch the first rows together from left to right and add the next row from right to left.

assemble quilt center

[1] Referring to photograph, *right*, lay out blocks in eight rows, turning every other block a quarter turn. Join blocks in each row. Press seams in one direction, alternating direction with each row.

[2] Join rows to make quilt center. Press seams in one direction. The quilt center should be 32½" square including seam allowances.

assemble and add borders

[1] Sew solid white 1¾×32½" inner border strips to opposite edges of quilt center. Add solid white 1¾×35" inner border strips to remaining edges. Press all seams toward inner border.

[2] Alternating color placement, lay out 12 solid white 2" squares and 11 assorted print 2" squares in a row. Join squares to make a short middle border strip.

The strip should be 2×35" including seam allowances. Repeat to make a second short middle border strip. Sew short middle border strips to opposite edges of quilt center. Press seams toward middle border.

[3] Alternating color placement, lay out 13 assorted print 2" squares and 12 solid white 2" squares in a row. Join squares to make a long middle border strip. The strip should be 2×38" including seam allowances. Repeat to make a second long middle border strip. Sew long middle border strips to remaining edges of quilt center. Press seams toward middle border.

[4] Sew solid white 3½×38" outer border strips to opposite edges of quilt center. Add solid white 3½×44" outer border strips to remaining edges to complete quilt top. Press all seams toward middle border.

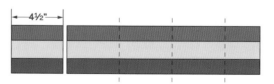

← 4½" →

STRIP SET DIAGRAM

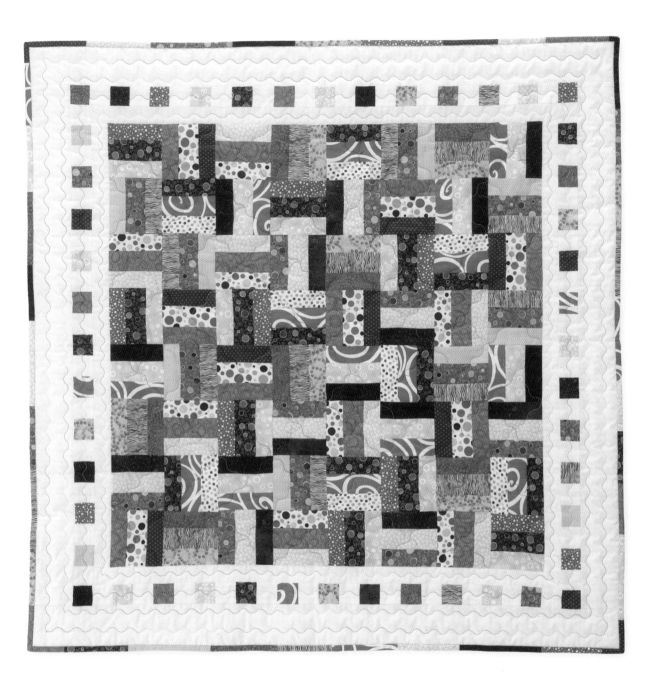

finish quilt

[1] Layer quilt top, batting, and backing; baste. (For details, see Complete the Quilt, *page 158*.)

[2] Quilt as desired. In the center, this quilt features a serpentine stitch (a wavy machine stitch) sewn in a diagonal grid with lines spaced 2½" apart. Four parallel serpentine stitched lines are sewn in the borders.

[3] Join the assorted print 2½"-wide strips into a 200"-long binding strip. Bind quilt with pieced strip. (For details, see Better Binding, *page 159*.)

cutie **pie**

Animal-head safety pin appliqués add fun pizzazz
to a wall quilt—and brighten Baby's room with
contagious smiles no one can resist.

DESIGNER **AMY BRADLEY**   MACHINE QUILTER **ROSIE MAYHEW**
PHOTOGRAPHER **ADAM ALBRIGHT**

materials

- 1⅝ yards purple dot (appliqué foundation, outer border, binding)
- ¼ yard white print (appliqués)
- ⅛ yard white tone-on-tone (appliqués)
- Scraps of assorted prints, dots, and solids in pink, blue, green, yellow, white, and orange (appliqués)
- ¼ yard dark purple print (inner border)
- ⅜ yard total assorted blue prints, dots, and stripes (middle border blocks)
- ⅜ yard total assorted pink prints, dots, and stripes (middle border blocks)
- 2—9×22" pieces (fat eighths) assorted yellow prints (middle border blocks)
- ⅛ yard multicolor stripe (middle border blocks)

- ⅓ yard muslin
- 2½ yards backing fabric
- 45" square batting
- 1½ yards 12"-wide lightweight fusible web
- Machine-embroidery thread: brown
- Embroidery floss: dark brown
- Clear acrylic ruler (optional)

Finished quilt: 39" square
Finished block: 6×12"

Quantities are for 44/45"-wide, 100% cotton fabrics.
Measurements include ¼" seam allowances. Sew with right sides together unless otherwise stated.

cut fabrics

Cut pieces in the following order (see Tip, *below*). Patterns are on *Pattern Sheet 1*. To use fusible web for appliquéing, complete the following steps.

[1] Lay fusible web, paper side up, over patterns. Use a pencil to trace each pattern the number of times indicated in cutting instructions, leaving ½" between tracings. Cut out each fusible-web shape roughly ¼" outside traced lines. Cut ¼" inside traced lines of each piece and discard centers (see Tip, *below*).

[2] Following manufacturer's instructions, press fusible-web shapes onto wrong sides of designated fabrics; let cool. Cut out fabric shapes on drawn lines. Peel off paper backings.

From purple dot, cut:
▸ 1—24½" square
▸ 5—2½×42" binding strips
▸ 2—1¾×39" outer border strips
▸ 2—1¾×36½" outer border strips

From white print, cut:
▸ 1 each of letters C, U, T, and P
▸ 2 of letter E

From white tone-on-tone, cut:
▸ 6 of Pattern A

From assorted scraps, cut:
▸ 1 each of patterns B, C, D, F, H, I, and J
▸ 2 of Pattern E

From dark purple print, cut:
▸ 2—1½×24½" inner border strips
▸ 2—1½×22½" inner border strips
▸ 1 of Pattern G

From assorted blue prints, dots, and stripes, cut:
▸ 2—6½×12½" rectangles
▸ 2—4½×10½" rectangles
▸ 8—1½×10½" strips (four sets of two matching strips)
▸ 8—1½×6½" strips (four sets of two matching strips)
▸ 1 of Pattern K

tip

Use a crafts knife and a rotary cutting mat to cut out interior spaces from letters and safety pin appliqués.

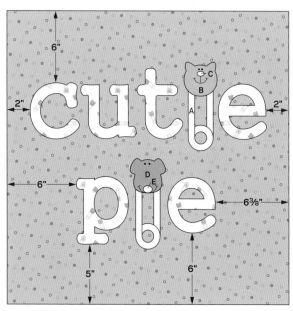

QUILT CENTER APPLIQUÉ PLACEMENT DIAGRAM

From assorted pink prints, dots, and stripes, cut:

▸ 2—6½×12½" rectangles
▸ 2—4½×10½" rectangles
▸ 8—1½×10½" strips (four sets of two matching strips)
▸ 8—1½×6½" strips (four sets of two matching strips)

From assorted yellow prints, cut:

▸ 2—4½×10½" rectangles

From multicolor stripe, cut:

▸ 4—1½×10½" strips
▸ 4—1½×6½" strips

appliqué quilt center

[1] Referring to **Quilt Center Appliqué Placement Diagram**, arrange white print letters, white tone-on-tone A safety pins, and

appliqué pieces B, C, D, and E on purple dot 24½" square appliqué foundation. Use clear acrylic ruler to align letters, if desired. Fuse pieces in place.

[2] Using brown thread, machine-blanket-stitch around edges of each piece, beginning with the bottom layer and working toward the top. Use straight stitches to add nose and smile lines (as marked) to cat and dog appliqués.

[3] Referring to photo on *page 49*, use dark brown floss and French knots to add eyes to each animal appliqué and make quilt center.

To make a French knot, refer to **French Knot Diagram** and pull thread through at point where knot is desired (A). Wrap thread around needle two or three times. Insert tip of needle into fabric at B, ¹⁄₁₆" away from A. Gently push wraps down needle to meet fabric. Pull needle and trailing thread through fabric slowly and smoothly.

FRENCH KNOT

[4] Trim quilt center to 22½" square.

add inner border

Sew short dark purple print inner border strips to opposite edges of quilt center. Sew long dark purple print inner border strips to remaining edges. Press all seams toward inner border.

assemble appliquéd units

[1] Referring to **Block Appliqué Placement Diagrams**, arrange white tone-on-tone A safety pin and F appliqué piece on an assorted blue print, dot, or stripe 6½×12½" rectangle. Fuse pieces in place.

[2] Using brown thread, machine-blanket-stitch around edges of each piece, beginning with the bottom layer and working toward the top. Use straight stitches to add smile (as marked) on appliqué.

[3] Referring to photo on *page 49* and using French knots, add eyes to appliqué to make one blue appliquéd unit.

[4] Trim unit to 4½×10½".

[5] Using appliqué pieces A, G, and H, repeat steps 1–4 to make a second blue appliquéd unit.

[6] Using remaining white tone-on-tone A safety pins, two assorted pink print, dot, or stripe 6½×12½" rectangles, and appliqué pieces I, J, K, and E, repeat steps 1–4 to make two pink appliquéd units. Use blanket stitches to add the curl to the chick (as marked).

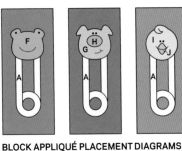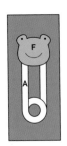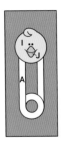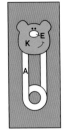

BLOCK APPLIQUÉ PLACEMENT DIAGRAMS

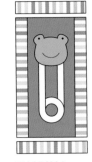

DIAGRAM 1

assemble and add middle border

[1] Referring to **Diagram 1**, sew matching blue print, dot, or stripe 1½×10½" strips to opposite edges of a blue appliquéd unit. Join matching blue print, dot, or stripe 1½×6½" strips to remaining edges to make a blue block. Press all seams toward blue strips. Blue block should be 6½×12½" including seam allowances.

[2] Using remaining blue appliquéd unit and the blue print, dot, or stripe 4½×10½" rectangles and 1½×6½" and 1½×10½" strips, repeat Step 1 to make four blue blocks total.

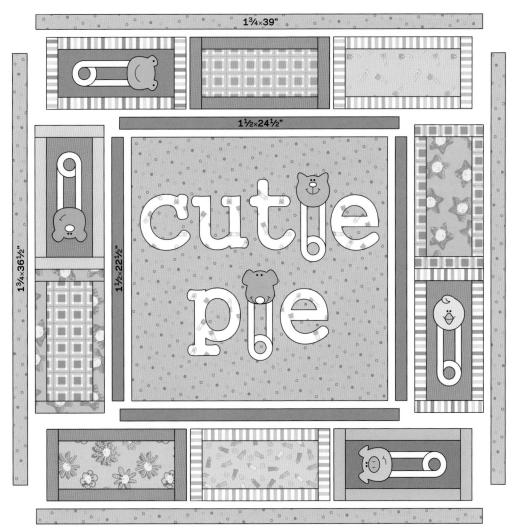

QUILT ASSEMBLY DIAGRAM

[3] Using two pink appliquéd units and the pink print, dot, or stripe 4½×10½" rectangles and 1½×6½" and 1½×10½" strips, repeat Step 1 to make four pink blocks total (**Diagram 2**).

[4] Using two assorted yellow print 4½×10½" rectangles and multicolor stripe 1½×6½" and 1½×10½" strips, repeat Step 1 to make two yellow blocks total (**Diagram 3**).

[5] Referring to **Quilt Assembly Diagram**, *page 51*, sew together an appliquéd pink block and a blue block to make a short middle border strip. Repeat to make a second short middle border strip. Press seams in one direction.

[6] Sew together an appliquéd blue block, a pink block, and a yellow block to make a long middle border strip. Repeat to make a second long middle border strip. Press seams in one direction.

[7] Sew short middle border strips to opposite edges of quilt center. Add long middle border strips to remaining edges. Press all seams toward inner border.

add outer border

Sew short purple dot outer border strips to opposite edges of quilt center. Sew long purple dot outer border strips to remaining edges to complete quilt top. Press all seams toward outer border.

finish quilt

[1] Layer quilt top, batting, and backing; baste. (For details, see Complete the Quilt, *page 158*.)

[2] Quilt as desired. This quilt was stippled across the quilt center (but not over the appliqués). A spiral design was stitched in the inner and outer borders, and a wavy design was added to the middle border blocks. A safety pin shape quilted in the center of the pink and blue blocks mimics the appliquéd shapes.

[3] Bind with purple dot binding strips. (For details, see Better Binding, *page 159*.)

tip

Test light-color appliqué fabrics by placing a dark foundation fabric behind them. If the dark fabric is visible, back appliqué fabrics with muslin before cutting out patterns. To back with muslin, iron a piece of fusible web to wrong side of fabric.

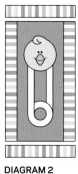

DIAGRAM 2

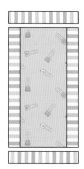

DIAGRAM 3

Welcome a baby girl with this more feminine version. Designer Amy Bradley simplified the design by selecting a three-color palette of pink, purple, and white prints, and used one flower appliqué across the quilt top instead of different animal appliqués. Amy chose one purple print for the flowers and one pink dot for the flower centers (**Block Appliqué Placement Diagram**). Patterns A, L, and M are on *Pattern Sheet 1*.

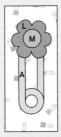

BLOCK APPLIQUÉ PLACEMENT DIAGRAM

Mix and match fabrics in primary colors and choose appliqués in the shape of a star, car, kite, or ball to personalize this for a special little boy. Or select themed fabrics, such as cowboy prints, and use appliqués in the shape of a horse or cowboy hat.

easy as

Showcase machine-embroidered alphabet blocks along two sides of this adorable, asymmetrical baby quilt.

DESIGNERS **CORI DERKSEN AND MYRA HARDER**   QUILTMAKER **KATHY WILLIAMS**
QUILTER **KAREN GILSON**   PHOTOGRAPHER **ANDY LYONS**

materials

- ▸ 1¼ yards blue toy print (blocks, outer border, binding)
- ▸ 1 yard blue crosshatch print (blocks, ABC and XYZ sections)
- ▸ ½ yard blue-and-white print (blocks)
- ▸ ½ yard blue alphabet print (blocks)
- ▸ ⅜ yard solid navy blue (inner border)
- ▸ ⅔ yard solid white (ABC and XYZ sections)
- ▸ ½ yard tear-away stabilizer
- ▸ Machine-embroidery thread: blue
- ▸ 2⅞ yards backing fabric
- ▸ 50×58" batting

Finished quilt: 43¼×51¾"   Finished block: 8" square

Quantities are for 44/45"-wide, 100% cotton fabrics. Measurements include ¼" seam allowances. Sew with right sides together unless otherwise stated.

cut fabrics

Cut pieces in the order that follows.

From blue toy print, cut:
- ▸ 5—3¼×42" strips for outer border
- ▸ 7—2½×42" strips for blocks and binding

From blue crosshatch print, cut:
- ▸ 2—2½×42" strips
- ▸ 2—3¼×25½" strips
- ▸ 2—3×23¾" strips
- ▸ 1—10¾×21" rectangle
- ▸ 3—3¼×5¾" rectangles
- ▸ 3—3×5¾" rectangles
- ▸ 1—1½×5¾" rectangle

From blue-and-white print, cut:
- ▸ 6—1½×8½" strips for position 8
- ▸ 12—1½×7½" strips for positions 6 and 7
- ▸ 12—1½×6½" strips for positions 4 and 5

- 12—1½×5½" strips for positions 2 and 3
- 6—1½×4½" strips for position 1

From blue alphabet print, cut:
- 6—1½×8½" strips for position 8
- 12—1½×7½" strips for positions 6 and 7
- 12—1½×6½" strips for positions 4 and 5
- 12—1½×5½" strips for positions 2 and 3
- 6—1½×4½" strips for position 1

From solid navy blue, cut:
- 5—1½×42" strips for inner border
- 1—1½×32½" strip
- 1—1½×25½" strip

From solid white, cut:
- 6—8" squares (these will be trimmed to 5¾" later)

assemble four-patch units

[1] Sew together a blue toy print 2½×42" strip and a blue crosshatch print 2½×42" strip to make a strip set (**Diagram 1**). Press seam toward blue crosshatch print. Repeat to make a second strip set.

[2] Cut strip sets into twenty-four 2½"-wide segments total.

[3] Join two 2½"-wide segments to make a four-patch unit (**Diagram 2**).

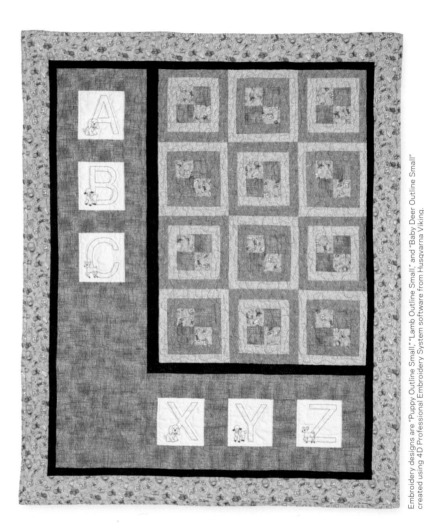

Embroidery designs are "Puppy Outline Small," "Lamb Outline Small," and "Baby Deer Outline Small" created using 4D Professional Embroidery System software from Husqvarna Viking.

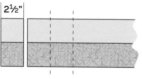

DIAGRAM 1

DIAGRAM 2

DIAGRAM 3

DIAGRAM 4

DIAGRAM 5

DIAGRAM 6

Press seam in one direction. The unit should be 4½" square including seam allowances. Repeat to make 12 four-patch units total.

assemble blocks

[1] Sew a blue-and-white print position 1 rectangle to left-hand edge of a four-patch unit (Diagram 3). Press seam toward white rectangle.

[2] Add a blue-and-white print position 2 rectangle to bottom edge of four-patch unit (Diagram 4). Press as before.

[3] Continue adding blue-and-white print rectangles and blue toy print rectangles in numerical order to make a Log Cabin block A (Diagram 5). Press all seams toward rectangles. The block should be 8½" square including seam allowances.

[4] Repeat steps 1 through 3 to make six total of Log Cabin block A.

[5] Referring to Diagram 6 and steps 1 through 3, use remaining four-patch units, blue alphabet print

rectangles, and blue-and-white print rectangles to make six total of Log Cabin block B.

embroider blocks

The alphabet blocks on this quilt were made using a computerized embroidery machine. Quiltmaker Kathy Williams used embroidery software to digitize a Helvetica font from her computer's font library for the letters. She then resized three animal designs from her software library and merged the letters and animals to create three designs for the block motifs.

color option

Mottled green "grass" grounds technicolor daisies on quilt tester Laura Boehnke's version of "Easy as ABC." The mix of large and medium prints with mottled tone-on-tone solids helps give the eye a place to rest. Laura pieced each outer border strip from five 3¼"-wide rectangles, alternating between large flowers, small blooms, and stylized squares. "This quilt actually reminds me of a gameboard," she says. "I can also envision it as a great 'I Spy' quilt for kids, using novelty prints in the 5¾" squares and four-patch units."

[1] Create A, B, C, and X, Y, Z embroidery motifs as desired. Scale the designs so each will stitch out in a space approximately 4½" to 4¾" square.

[2] Layer an 8" square of stabilizer beneath the wrong side of a solid white 8" square. Using blue embroidery thread and centering the motif, machine embroider each design. Gently remove the stabilizer. Centering the motifs, trim each block to 5¾" square.

assemble quilt center

[1] Referring to **Quilt Assembly Diagram**, lay out Log Cabin blocks in four rows, alternating A and B blocks.

[2] Sew together blocks in each row. Press seams toward A blocks.

[3] Join rows to make Log Cabin section. Press seams in one direction. The Log Cabin section should be 24½×32½" including seam allowances.

[4] Sew solid navy 1½×32½" strip to left-hand edge of Log Cabin section. Add solid navy 1½×25½" strip to bottom edge. Press all seams toward navy strips.

[5] Referring to **Quilt Assembly Diagram**, join three blue check 3×5¾" rectangles and the A, B, and C 5¾" squares in a vertical row. Press seams toward blue crosshatch print. Add blue crosshatch print 3×23¾" strips to long edges to make ABC section. Press seams toward blue check strips.

[6] Referring to **Quilt Assembly Diagram**, join a blue crosshatch print 1½×5¾" rectangle, three blue crosshatch print 3¼×5¾" rectangles, and the X, Y, and Z 5¾" squares in a horizontal row. Press seams toward blue check rectangles. Sew blue crosshatch print 3¼×25½" strips to long edges to make XYZ section. Press seams toward blue crosshatch print strips.

[7] Referring to **Quilt Assembly Diagram**, join ABC section, blue crosshatch print 10¾×21" rectangle, Log Cabin section, and XYZ section in two vertical rows. Press seams in one direction. Join rows to make quilt center; press seam in one direction. The quilt center should be 35¾×44¼" including seam allowances.

add borders

[1] Cut and piece solid navy 1½×42" strips to make:
  ▸ 2—1½×44¼" inner border strips
  ▸ 2—1½×37¾" inner border strips

[2] Sew long inner border strips to long edges of quilt center. Add short inner border strips to remaining edges. Press all seams toward inner border.

[3] Cut and piece blue toy print 3¼×42" strips to make:
  ▸ 2—3¼×46¼" outer border strips
  ▸ 2—3¼×43¼" outer border strips

[4] Sew long outer border strips to opposite edges of quilt center. Add short outer border strips to remaining edges to complete quilt top. Press all seams toward outer border.

finish quilt

[1] Layer quilt top, batting, and backing. (For details, see Complete the Quilt, *page 158*.)

[2] Quilt as desired.

[3] Bind with blue toy print binding strips. (For details, see Better Binding, *page 159*.)

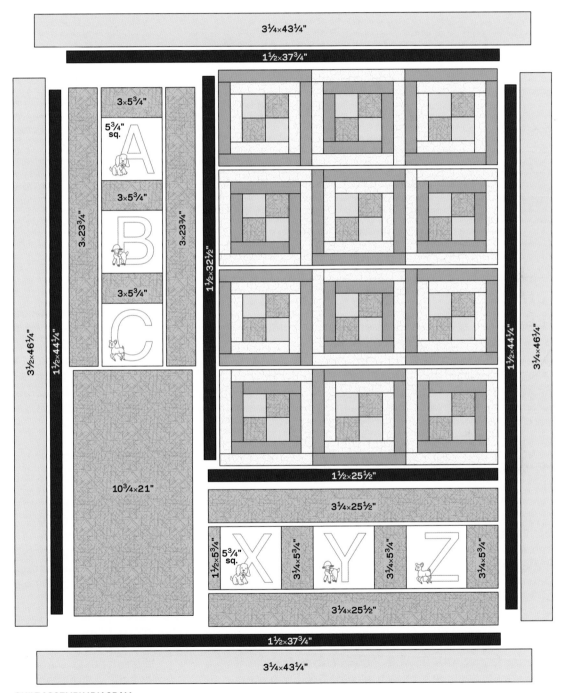

QUILT ASSEMBLY DIAGRAM

whirly bird

Fast, fun, and fusible—
you'll finish this irresistible baby quilt in a flash.

DESIGNER **AMY BRADLEY**   MACHINE QUILTER **ROSIE MAYHEW**
PHOTOGRAPHER **GREG SCHEIDEMANN**

materials

- 21×36½" piece blue polka dot (appliqué foundation)
- ½ yard purple print (appliqué, binding)
- ⅛ yard pink polka dot (appliqués)
- ⅛ yard yellow print (appliqués, piping)
- 2" square white polka dot (appliqués)
- Scrap each of solid white, solid cream, yellow geometric, and green and orange prints (appliqués)
- Scraps of assorted purple prints (appliqués)
- ½ yard multicolor squares print (border)
- 1¾ yards backing fabric
- 31×47" batting
- 1 yard lightweight fusible web
- ⅛ yard tear-away fabric stabilizer
- Machine embroidery thread: black, white
- Embroidery floss: black
- Black seed beads
- 1" diameter button: orange
- 2—¾"-diameter buttons: purple

Finished quilt: 24¾×40"

Quantities are for 44/45"-wide, 100% cotton fabrics.
Measurements include ¼" seam allowances. Sew with right sides together unless otherwise stated.

cut fabrics

Cut pieces in the following order. Patterns are on *Pattern Sheet 3*. To use fusible web for appliquéing, complete the following steps. (For more information on fusible appliqué, see Piece and Appliqué, *page 155*.)

[1] Lay fusible web, paper side up, over patterns. Use a pencil to trace each pattern the number of times indicated in cutting instructions, leaving ½" between tracings. Cut out each fusible-web shape roughly ¼" outside traced lines.

[2] Following manufacturer's instructions, press fusible-web shapes onto wrong sides of designated fabrics; let cool. Cut out fabric shapes on drawn lines. Peel off paper backings.

applique quilt center

From purple print, cut:
- 4—2½×42" binding strips
- 1 of Pattern S

From pink polka dot, cut:
- 1 each of patterns B and X

From yellow print, cut:
- 2—1×33½" strips
- 2—1×18¼" strips
- 1 each of patterns E, M, Q, and U

From white polka dot, cut:
- 1 each of patterns BB and CC

From solid white, cut:
- 1 each of patterns J and V

From solid cream, cut:
- 1 each of patterns F, H, and K

From yellow geometric, cut:
- 1 each of patterns R and AA

From green print, cut:
- 1 each of patterns A, O, P, Y, and Z

From orange print, cut:
- 1 each of patterns G, I, and L
- 2 of Pattern AA

From assorted purple prints, cut:
- 3 of Pattern AA
- 1 each of patterns C, D, N, T, and W

From multicolor squares print, cut:
- 2—3¾×33½" border strips
- 2—3¾×24¾" border strips
- 3 of Pattern AA

From fabric stabilizer, cut:
- 1—2×20" strip
- 1 of Pattern DD

[1] Lay out pieces A through CC on blue polka dot 21×36½" rectangle (**Appliqué Placement Diagram**). When you are pleased with the arrangement, fuse in place. Note: When appliquéing, shadows may show through some fabrics, especially if the foundation fabric is darker than the appliqué fabric. Amy suggests testing all appliqué fabrics before cutting by placing a dark fabric behind them. If the dark fabric is visible, you may need to back the appliqué fabric with muslin.

To do this, iron a piece of fusible web to the wrong side of the appliqué fabric. Peel paper off the back and fuse to muslin. Check the fabric again; some fabrics may need to be double-backed or may need a heavier muslin behind them.

tip

How many ladder rungs you need will depend on the number of letters in the name you use to personalize the quilt. Add 2½" of length per letter to the background and borders if the name is longer than eight letters.

[2] With black thread, machine-blanket-stitch around each appliqué, beginning with bottom layer and working toward the top.

[3] Referring to **Appliqué Placement Diagram** and photo on *page 63*, use black thread to machine-straight-stitch a smile and a nose on the face and strands of hair on top of the head. Use black embroidery floss to add two black seed beads for eyes. Amy suggests using a tear-away fabric stabilizer (or white muslin) DD piece under the foundation fabric when machine-stitching hair. To give the nose a slight blush, color softly with a light pink colored pencil.

[4] Referring to **Appliqué Placement Diagram** and photo for placement, position the 2×20" strip of stabilizer under the foundation fabric. Machine-satin-stitch letters between ladder rungs (see Tip). Use white thread to machine-satin-stitch sides of ladder.

[5] Trim appliqué foundation to 18¼×33½" including seam allowances to make quilt center.

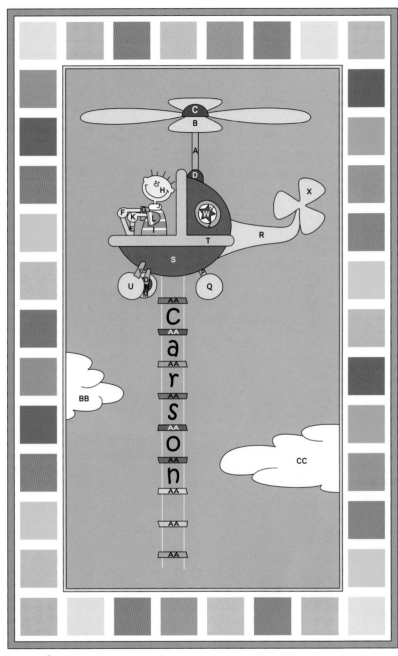

APPLIQUÉ PLACEMENT DIAGRAM

add piping

[1] With wrong sides together, fold each yellow print strip in half lengthwise to make piping strips; press.

[2] Aligning raw edges, sew long piping strips to long edges of quilt center. Sew short piping strips

to remaining edges. Quilt center is still 18¼×33½" including seam allowances.

add border

Sew 3¾×33½" multicolor squares print border strips to long edges of quilt center. Sew 3¾×24¾" multicolor squares print border strips to remaining edges to complete quilt top. Press all seams toward border.

finish quilt

[1] Layer quilt top, batting, and backing; baste. (For details, see Complete the Quilt, *page 158*.)

[2] Quilt as desired. This quilt features machine-quilted clouds across the quilt center and echo-quilting around the appliqués. A wavy line runs along the inside of the border and crisscrosses through the colorful printed squares of the border.

[3] Bind with purple print binding strips. (For details, see Better Binding, *page 159*.)

[4] Sew a purple button on each helicopter wheel and an orange button on the tail propeller.

color cubes

Add a handmade touch of wonder for Baby by sewing a dozen or more of these soft, poly-fiber-filled play blocks.

DESIGNER **JEANNE PRYOR** PHOTOGRAPHER **GREG SCHEIDEMANN**

materials

- Scraps of assorted prints, stripes, and solids (blocks, optional appliqués)
- Polyester fiberfill
- Fusible web (optional)

Finished block:
2½" cube

Measurements include ¼" seam allowances. Sew with right sides together unless otherwise stated.

cut fabrics

Cut pieces in the following order. Pattern is on *Pattern Sheet 2*.

To make and use a template for cutting the Cube Pattern, see Make and Use Templates on *page 154*. Be sure to transfer the dots (matching points) marked on the pattern to the template, then to the fabric pieces. The following instructions result in one block.

From assorted prints, stripes, and solids, cut:
▸ 6 of Cube Pattern

fuse the shapes and letters

Alhough designer Jeanne Pryor hand-appliquéd her blocks, you can personalize your blocks by adding a contrasting half circle, quarter circle, or letter to a side or two using our simplified fusible appliqué technique.

Half circle, quarter circle, and alphabet patterns are on *Pattern Sheet 2*. To use fusible web for cutting appliqué shapes, complete the following steps.

[1] Lay fusible web, paper side up, over patterns. Use a pencil to trace patterns, leaving at least ½" between tracings. Cut out fusible-web shapes roughly ¼" outside traced lines.

[2] Following manufacturer's instructions, press fusible-web shapes onto backs of desired fabrics. Let cool, then cut out shapes on drawn lines; peel off paper backings.

[3] Press fusible-web appliqués onto 3" fabric squares. Use a zigzag stitch to machine-appliqué pieces in place.

assemble block

[1] Referring to **Diagram 1**, sew together four squares, stopping and starting each seam at marked dots, ¼" from corners.

[2] Matching dots, sew another square to one edge of pieced unit (**Diagram 2**).

[3] Repeat Step 2, joining remaining square to unsewn edge of pieced unit, leaving a 1½" opening along one side for turning, to make a cube (**Diagram 3**).

[4] Turn cube right side out. Stuff with fiberfill to desired firmness, working fiberfill into corners. Using quilting thread or doubled thread, securely hand-sew opening together to complete the block.

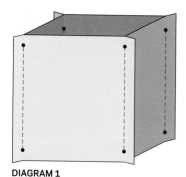

DIAGRAM 1

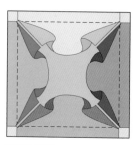

DIAGRAM 2

Leave open

DIAGRAM 3

kids

Whether your child is a free spirit, an adventurer, or always on the go, this collection of bright and cheery quilts, pillows, wall hangings, and more are certain to be a hit among boys and girls alike.

i spy...

In no time you can create an interactive quilt using a playful mix of prints that reflect a few of your child's favorite things.

DESIGNER **KAREN MONTGOMERY**   QUILTMAKER **KATE HARDY**   QUILTER **NANCY SHARR**
PHOTOGRAPHER **ANDY LYONS AND CRAIG ANDERSON**

materials

- ⅜ yard each of mottled lime green, mottled teal, mottled red, and mottled blue (appliqué foundations)
- 16—7" squares of novelty prints, 4 each with backgrounds in lime green, teal, red, and blue (magnifying glass appliqués)
- ⅛ yard each of mottled black and mottled gray (handle appliqués)
- 1⅓ yards bug stripe print (sashing)
- ½ yard mottled green (binding)
- 2⅞ yards backing fabric
- 51×72" batting
- Lightweight fusible web
- Black thread

Finished quilt: 44½×65½"   Finished block: 8×11"

Quantities are for 44/45"-wide, 100% cotton fabrics. Measurements include a ¼" seam allowance. Sew with right sides together unless otherwise stated.

cut fabrics

To make the best use of your fabrics, cut pieces in the following order. Cut sashing strips lengthwise (parallel to the selvage).

Patterns are on *Pattern Sheet 1*. To use fusible web for appliquéing, complete the following steps. (For more information on fusible appliqué, see Piece & Appliqué, *page 155*.)

[1] Lay fusible web, paper side up, over patterns A and B. Use a pencil to trace each pattern 16 times, leaving ½" between tracings. Cut out each fusible-web shape roughly ¼" outside the traced lines.

[2] Following the manufacturer's instructions, press fusible-web shapes onto backs of designated fabrics; let cool. Cut out fabric shapes on drawn lines and peel off paper backings.

From each mottled lime green, teal, red, and blue piece, cut:
▸ 4—8½×11½" rectangles
From each novelty print square, cut:
▸ 1 of Pattern A
From mottled black, cut:
▸ 12 of Pattern B
From mottled gray, cut:
▸ 4 of Pattern B
From bug stripe print, cut:
▸ 2—8×44½" sashing strips
▸ 3—6½×44½" sashing strips
From mottled green, cut:
▸ 6—2½×42" binding strips

appliqué blocks

[1] Using a quilter's pencil, mark a point 1½" down from the upper left-hand corner and ½" up from the lower right-hand corner of a mottled lime green 8½×11½" rectangle (**Diagram 1**). Connect points to make an appliqué foundation with a placement line.

[2] Fold a lime green novelty print A circle in half. Lightly finger-press the fold to mark the center; unfold. Fold a mottled black B handle in half lengthwise; finger-press, then unfold.

[3] Place prepared A circle 1½" from the left-hand edge of the prepared mottled lime green foundation, aligning circle center line with marked placement line (**Diagram 2**). Center prepared B handle over placement line with handle end ¼" from the circle. Fuse both pieces in place.

[4] Using black thread, machine-blanket-stitch around handle. Machine-satin-stitch on the marked diagonal line between handle and circle, then around circle to complete a lime green A block.

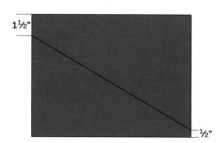

DIAGRAM 1

DIAGRAM 2

DIAGRAM 3

[5] Repeat steps 1 through 4 to make a second lime green A block.

[6] Using matching-color rectangles and novelty print circle appliqués, repeat steps 1 through 4 to make two teal A blocks, two red A blocks, and two blue A blocks; use mottled gray handles for the blue A blocks.

[7] Reversing the direction of the placement line, repeat steps 1 through 4 to make two lime green B blocks (**Diagram 3**), two teal B blocks, two red B blocks, and two blue B blocks; use the mottled gray handles for the blue B blocks.

tip

Consider these other "I Spy" quilt themes: sports, zoo/safari, birds, flowers, shapes and colors, photo transfer, dinosaurs, trucks/diggers, dogs, and cats.

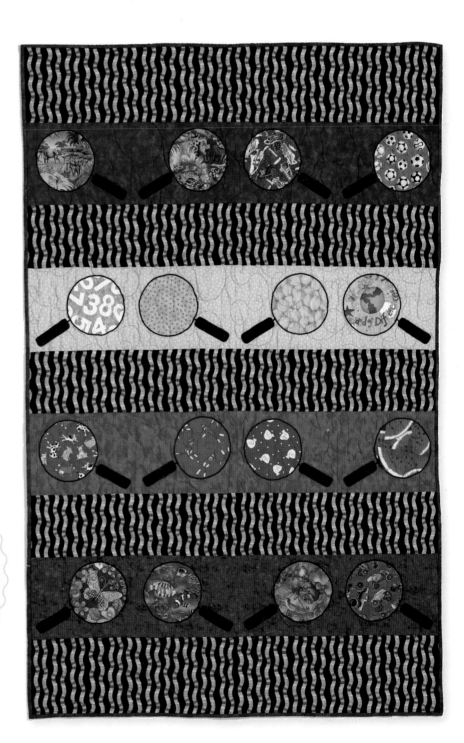

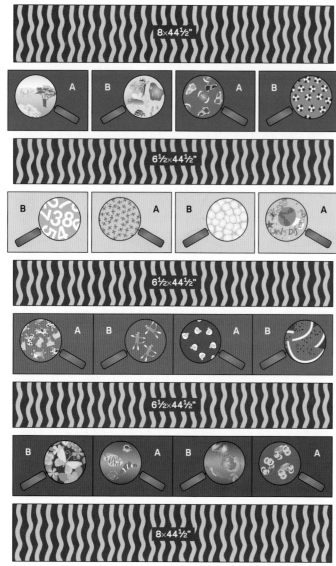

QUILT ASSEMBLY DIAGRAM

assemble quilt top

[1] Referring to **Quilt Assembly Diagram**, lay out A and B blocks, bug stripe print 6½×44½" sashing strips, and bug stripe print 8×44½" sashing strips in rows.

[2] Sew together pieces in each row; press seams in one direction. Join rows to complete quilt top. Press seams in one direction.

finish quilt

[1] Layer quilt top, batting, and backing; baste. (For details, see Complete the Quilt, *page 158.*)

[2] Quilt as desired. Machine-quilter Barb Kiester stitched an allover loop in each block background, adding stitched bug outlines randomly. She also stitched ¼" and 2" from the edge on each magnifying glass.

[3] Bind with mottled green binding strips. (For details, see Better Binding, *page 159.*)

color option

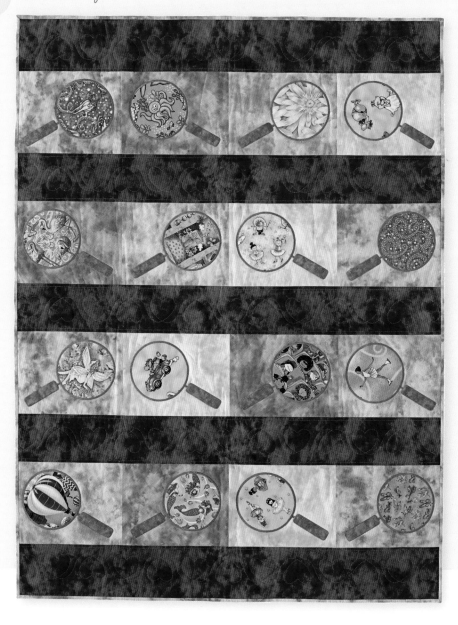

Little girls can spy things they love in a pretty version of "I Spy" that takes a slightly different twist. Instead of using the same background for all the blocks in a row, mix up the backgrounds for a more playful look.

dino *might!*

Kids will love to see
the appliquéd dinosaur come back to life
on a simple graphic background.

DESIGNERS **CORI DERKSEN AND MYRA HARDER** PHOTOGRAPHER **MARTY BALDWIN**

materials

- ▸ 11×17" piece mottled turquoise (appliqué foundation)
- ▸ 1⅛ yards mottled brown (appliqué foundation)
- ▸ 5—5×12" pieces assorted prints in turquoise, light turquoise, brown, and cream (appliqué foundation)
- ▸ 1 yard brown polka dot (appliqué foundation, border, binding)
- ▸ ⅔ yard light turquoise print (dinosaur appliqué)
- ▸ Scrap of solid dark brown (eye appliqué)
- ▸ 2⅝ yards backing fabric
- ▸ 46×52" batting
- ▸ Lightweight fusible web
- ▸ Matching or monofilament thread

Finished quilt: 39½×45½"

Quantities are for 44/45"-wide, 100% cotton fabrics. Measurements include ¼" seam allowances. Sew with right sides together unless otherwise stated.

cut fabrics

Cut pieces in the following order. The patterns are on *Pattern Sheet 2.*

To use fusible web for appliquéing, complete the following steps. (For more information on fusible appliqué, see Piece and Appliqué, *page 155*.)

[1] Lay fusible web, paper side up, over patterns. Use a pencil to trace each pattern once, leaving ½" between tracings. Cut out each fusible-web shape roughly ¼" outside traced lines.

[2] Following manufacturer's instructions, press fusible-web shapes onto wrong sides of designated fabrics; let cool. Cut out fabric shapes on drawn lines. Peel off paper backings.

From mottled turquoise, cut:
▸ 1—9½×15½" rectangle

From mottled brown, cut:
▸ 2—6½×33½" strips
▸ 2—6½×27½" strips
▸ 6—3½×15½" rectangles

From each assorted print, cut:
▸ 3—3½" squares

From brown polka dot, cut:
▸ 5—2½×42" binding strips
▸ 4—3½×39½" border strips
▸ 3—3½" squares

From light turquoise print, cut:
▸ 1 of Pattern A

From solid dark brown, cut:
▸ 1 of Pattern B

assemble quilt center

[1] Sew mottled brown 3½×15½" rectangles to long edges of mottled turquoise 9½×15½" rectangle (Diagram 1).

Join mottled brown 3½×15½" rectangles to remaining edges. Press all seams toward mottled brown rectangles.

[2] Referring to **Diagram 2**, sew together a mottled brown 3½×15½" rectangle and two assorted print 3½" squares to make a side pieced strip. Press seams in one direction. The side pieced strip should be 3½×21½" including seam allowances. Repeat to make a second side pieced strip. Sew pieced strips to long edges of Step 1 unit. Press seams toward pieced strips.

[3] Join seven assorted print and brown polka dot 3½" squares to make top pieced strip (Diagram 2). Press seams in one direction. The strip should be 3½×21½" including seam allowances. Repeat to make bottom pieced strip. Sew top and bottom pieced strips to remaining edges of Step 1 unit.

[4] Sew mottled brown 6½×27½" strips to long edges of Step 3 unit. Join mottled brown 6½×33½" strips to remaining edges to make appliqué foundation. Press all seams toward

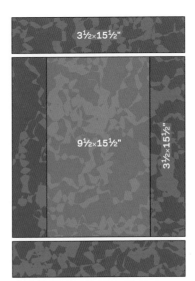

3½×15½"

9½×15½"

3½×15½"

DIAGRAM 1

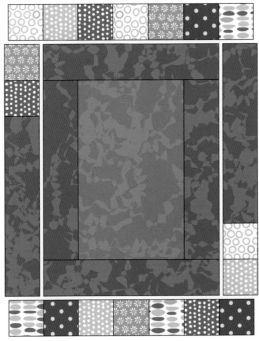

DIAGRAM 2

mottled brown strips. The appliqué foundation should be 33½×39½" including seam allowances.

appliqué quilt center

Referring to **Quilt Assembly Diagram**, position light turquoise print A dinosaur and dark brown B eye on appliqué foundation; fuse in place. Using matching thread or monofilament thread, machine-appliqué around each appliqué shape.

add border

Sew brown polka dot 3½×39½" border strips to long edges of appliqué foundation. Join brown polka dot 3½×39½" border strips to remaining edges to complete quilt top. Press all seams toward border.

finish quilt

[1] Layer quilt top, batting, and backing; baste. (For details, see Complete the Quilt, *page 158*.)

[2] Quilt as desired. This quilt is machine-quilted with outline stitching around the dinosaur and parallel vertical lines running through it. An X is quilted through each assorted print

QUILT ASSEMBLY DIAGRAM

square. The remainder of the quilt top features a large circle motif in varying sizes.

[3] Bind with brown polka dot binding strips. (For details, see Better Binding, *page 159*.)

tip

To reduce the stiffness of a finished appliqué project, cut away the center of each fusible-web shape ¼" inside the traced lines and discard the center before fusing the shape to the back of the appliqué fabric.

hide&seek

Made to entertain, this colorful throw will keep little hands and young minds busy—great for visits to Grandma's house or a rainy afternoon.

DESIGNER **JOLYN OLSON** PHOTOGRAPHERS **GREG SCHEIDEMANN, MARTY BALDWIN AND MARCIA CAMERON**

materials

- ⅞ yard blue stripe (blocks)
- 2⅓ yards light blue print (blocks)
- 99—3" squares assorted novelty prints (blocks)
- 1½ yards blue-and-red stripe (blocks, binding)
- 1⅛ yards red print (border)
- 3½ yards backing fabric
- 62×72" batting

Finished quilt: 55½×65½" Finished block: 5" square

Quantities are for 44/45"-wide, 100% cotton fabrics. Measurements include ¼" seam allowances. Sew with right sides together unless otherwise stated.

cut fabrics

To make the best use of your fabrics, cut pieces in the following order.

For each stripe fabric, cut half of the 2⅛" squares diagonally from the bottom left corner to the top right corner; cut remaining squares diagonally from the bottom right corner to the top left corner.

To make block assembly easier, read through the instructions and study the diagrams before you begin to sew.

From blue stripe, cut:
- 200—2⅛" squares, cutting each in half diagonally for 400 triangles total (place stripes in same direction)

From light blue print, cut:
- 396—2⅛" squares, cutting each in half diagonally for 792 triangles total
- 396—1¾" squares

From blue-and-red stripe, cut:
- 1—18×42" rectangle, cut into enough 2½"-wide bias strips to total 264" for binding (For details, see Cutting on the Bias, *page 158*.)
- 96—2⅛" squares, cutting each in half diagonally for 392 triangles total (place stripes in same direction)

From red print, cut:
- 6—5½×42" strips for border

kids **79**

assemble blocks

[1] Sew together one blue stripe triangle (with stripes running vertically) and one light blue print triangle to make a triangle-square (**Diagram 1**). Press seam toward blue stripe triangle. The triangle-square should be 1¾" square including seam allowances. Repeat to make four triangle-squares total.

[2] Repeat Step 1, using four blue stripe triangles (with stripes running horizontally) to make four additional triangle-squares (**Diagram 2**).

[3] Lay out the eight triangle-squares, four light blue print 1¾" squares, and one novelty print 3" square in rows (**Diagram 3**; note orientation of stripes in triangle-squares).

[4] Sew together pieces in each row. Press seams toward squares. Join rows to make a blue Ohio Star block (**Diagram 4**). Press seams in one direction. The block should be 5½" square including seam allowances. Repeat to make 50 blue Ohio Star blocks total.

[5] Repeat steps 1 through 4 using eight blue-and-red stripe triangles (four in each stripe orientation), eight light blue print triangles, four light blue print 1¾" squares, and one novelty print 3" square to make a blue-and-red Ohio Star block. Refer to **Diagram 5** for placement of stripes. Repeat to make 49 blue-and-red Ohio Star blocks total.

assemble quilt center

[1] Lay out 99 Ohio Star blocks in rows, alternating blue and blue-and-red blocks (**Quilt Assembly Diagram**).

[2] Sew together blocks in each row. Press seams in one direction, alternating direction with each row. Join rows to make quilt center. Press seams in one direction. The quilt center should be 45½x55½" including seam allowances.

add border

[1] Cut and piece red print 5½x42" strips to make:
   ▸ 4—5½x55½" border strips

[2] Sew border strips to long edges of quilt center. Join remaining border strips to remaining edges to complete quilt top. Press all seams toward border.

finish quilt

[1] Layer quilt top, batting, and backing; baste. (For details, see Complete the Quilt, *page 158*.)

[2] Quilt as desired. Each star was stitched in the ditch, and the border was stitched with a diagonal 2" grid.

[3] Use blue-and-red stripe bias binding strips to bind quilt. (For details, see Better Binding, *page 159*.)

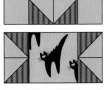

DIAGRAM 1

DIAGRAM 2　　**DIAGRAM 3**

DIAGRAM 4　　**DIAGRAM 5**

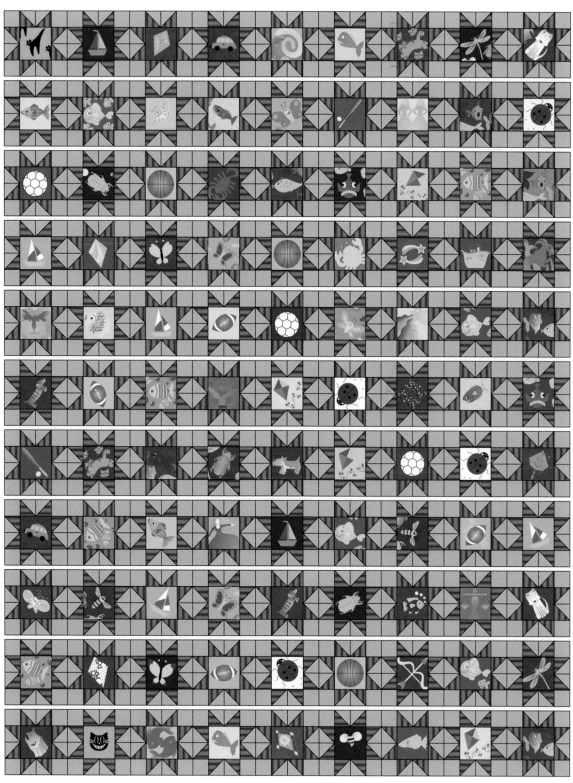

QUILT ASSEMBLY DIAGRAM

crayon *farm*

Become a kid again when
you color these cute designs on fabric.

DESIGNER **LAURENE SINEMA**   PHOTOGRAPHER **PERRY STRUSE**

materials

- ▸ 1 yard of muslin for stitchery foundations
- ▸ ⅞ yard of green check for border and binding
- ▸ 1¼ yards of backing fabric
- ▸ 41" square of quilt batting
- ▸ Freezer paper
- ▸ Crayons
- ▸ Typing paper or white paper towels
- ▸ Embroidery floss: black

Finished Quilt: 34½" square

Quantities are for 44/45"-wide, 100% cotton fabrics.
Measurements include ¼" seam allowances. Sew with
right sides together unless otherwise stated.

cut fabrics

Cut pieces in the following
order. Embroidery patterns
are on *Pattern Sheet 4.*

From muslin, cut:
- ▸ 1—11×17" rectangle
- ▸ 4—5×17" rectangles
- ▸ 4—6½×9½" rectangles
- ▸ 4—5¾×6½" rectangles

From green check, cut:
- ▸ 4—2½×42" binding strips
- ▸ 2—3½×35" border strips
- ▸ 2—3½×29" border strips

embellish blocks

[1] Cut freezer-paper
rectangles in the same
sizes as the muslin
rectangles. Using a warm,
dry iron, press each
freezer-paper rectangle
shiny side down to a
corresponding muslin
rectangle.

[2] Secure the barn embroidery
pattern to a light box or
other light source. Using a
quilter's pencil, trace the
picture onto the center of
the muslin 11×17" rectangle.

[3] Follow the instructions in
Step 2 to transfer the
chicken and duck embroidery
patterns to two of the
muslin 5×17" rectangles.
On a remaining muslin
5×17" rectangle, trace the
tulip embroidery pattern
five times (see the **Quilt
Assembly Diagram** on
page 84).
   Repeat to trace the corn
embroidery pattern five
times on the remaining
muslin 5x17" rectangle.

[4] Follow the instructions in Step 2 to transfer the cow, pig, sheep, and horse embroidery patterns to the four muslin 6½×9½" rectangles.

[5] Folllow the instructions in Step 2 to transfer the turkey, goat No. 1, cat and dog, and goat no. 2 embroidery patterns to the four muslin 5¾×6½" rectangles.

[6] Color the designs with crayons, then remove the freezer paper. Place one colored muslin rectangle right side up on your ironing board and cover the design with typing paper or a white paper towel. Press with a hot, dry iron to set the colors. Replace the typing paper or paper towel as needed to absorb as much of the wax as possible. If desired, add more color with crayons and press again.

[7] Using two strands of black embroidery floss and a running stitch, stitch each farm scene. To make a running stitch, pull your needle up at A and insert it into the fabric at B (**Running Stitch Diagram** on *page 84*). Continue in the same manner.

[8] Make French knots for the eyes on the animals. To make a French knot, bring your needle up through the fabric (**French Knot Diagram**). Wrap the floss around the needle twice without twisting it. Insert the needle back into the fabric 1/16" away from where you started. Gently push the wrap down the needle to meet the fabric, then pull then needle and floss through the fabric smoothly.

assemble quilt center

[1] Referring to **Quilt Assembly Diagram**, lay out the embellished muslin rectangles in three vertical rows.

[2] Sew together the blocks in each row. Press the seam allowances in one direction, alternating the direction with each row.

[3] Join the rows to complete the quilt center. Press the seam allowances in one direction. The pieced quilt center should measure 29" square, including the seam allowances.

add borders

[1] Sew the green check 3½×29" border strips to opposite edges of the pieced quilt center. Press the seam allowances toward the border.

[2] Join the green check 3½×35" border strips to the remaining edges of the pieced quilt center to complete the quilt top. Press the seam allowances toward the border.

finish quilt

[1] Layer quilt top, batting, and backing; baste. (For details, see Complete the Quilt, *page 158*.)

[2] Quilt as desired. This quilt was hand-quilted in the ditch of the block seams and around each drawn motif. A cable design is stitched in the border.

[3] Bind with green check binding strips. (For details, see Better Binding, *page 159*.)

RUNNING STITCH

FRENCH KNOT

QUILT ASSEMBLY DIAGRAM

Large, bright and cheery squares combine to make
this the perfect project for the first-time quilter.

QUILTER **NANCY SHARR** PHOTOGRAPHERS **ADAM ALBRIGHT AND MARTY BALDWIN**

kidding
around

materials

- ⅞ yard each orange print, blue print, and red print (squares)
- 1⅛ yards total assorted tan prints (squares)
- ⅞ yard total assorted brown prints (squares)
- ⅝ yard light tan print (squares)
- 1⅛ yards total assorted green prints (squares)
- ⅝ yard multicolor stripe (binding)
- 4⅛ yards backing fabric
- 73" square batting

Finished quilt: 67" square   Finished square: 9½" square

Quantities are for 44/45"-wide, 100% cotton fabrics. Measurements include ¼" seam allowances. Sew with right sides together unless otherwise stated.

cut fabrics

Cut pieces in the following order.

From orange print, cut:
- 5—10" squares

From blue print, cut:
- 5—10" squares

From red print, cut:
- 5—10" squares

From assorted tan prints, cut:
- 11—10" squares

From assorted brown prints, cut:
- 7—10" squares

From light tan print, cut:
- 4—10" squares

From assorted green prints, cut:
- 12—10" squares

From multicolor stripe, cut:
- 7—2½×42" strips for binding

assemble quilt top

[1] Referring to photo for placement, lay out orange, blue, tan, brown, light tan, red, and green print 10" squares in seven rows.

[2] Sew together squares in each row. Press seams in one direction, alternating direction with each row.

[3] Join rows to complete quilt top. Press seams in one direction.

finish quilt

[1] Layer quilt top, batting, and backing; baste. (For details, see Complete the Quilt, *page 158.*)

[2] Quilt as desired. This quilt was stitched with meandering loops across the quilt top.

[3] Bind with multicolor stripe binding strips. (For details, see Better Binding, *page 159.*)

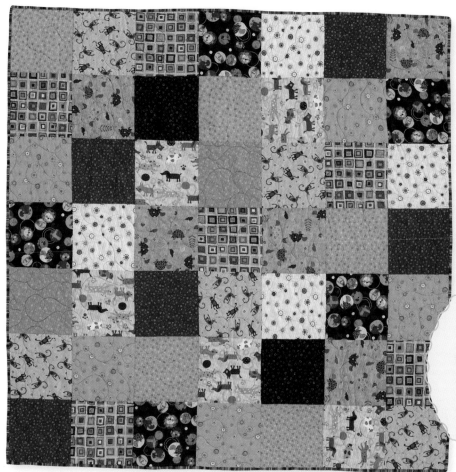

tip

To ease in a bit of extra fullness when the lengths of two pieced rows don't quite match, sew with the longer strip on the bottom against the machine bed.

color option

Use the floor or a design wall to play around with the position of the 10" squares. In this version, polka dots, circles, and paisleys blend for a more feminine throw.

kids' carryall

Stitch up a take-along bag that's the perfect size for kids to take on the run.

DESIGNER **CINDY TAYLOR OATES**   PHOTOGRAPHERS **KRITSADA AND GREG SCHEIDEMANN**

materials

- ▸ 9×22" piece (fat eighth) orange plaid (triangle-squares)
- ▸ 9×22" piece (fat eighth) orange print (triangle-squares)
- ▸ 18×22" piece (fat quarter) multicolor dot (band, bag base)
- ▸ ⅝ yard blue floral (squares, handles, lining)
- ▸ ½ yard muslin (backing)
- ▸ 16×26" thin batting
- ▸ 3×9" rectangle heavyweight cardboard

Finished bag: 9×9×3"

Quantities are for 44/45"-wide, 100% cotton fabrics. Measurements include ¼" seam allowances. Sew with right sides together unless otherwise stated.

tip

When choosing fabrics for the triangle-squares, select mostly small-scale prints. If you want a more secure bag, add a closure, such as ribbon ties, a button and loop, or magnetic snaps.

cut fabrics

Cut pieces in the following order.

From orange plaid, cut:
- ▸ 20—2⅜" squares

From orange print, cut:
- ▸ 20—2⅜" squares

From multicolor dot, cut:
- ▸ 1—3½×9½" rectangle
- ▸ 2—2×12½" rectangles

From blue floral, cut:
- ▸ 2—2×18½" strips for handles
- ▸ 2—9½×12½" rectangles
- ▸ 1—3½×9½" rectangle
- ▸ 40—2" squares

From muslin, cut:
- ▸ 2—9½×12½" rectangles
- ▸ 1—3½×9½" rectangle

From thin batting, cut:
- ▸ 2—9½×12½" rectangles
- ▸ 1—3½×9½" rectangle

assemble triangle-squares

[1] Use a pencil to mark a diagonal line on wrong side of each orange plaid 2⅜" square. (To prevent fabric from stretching as you draw lines, place 220-grit sandpaper under the squares.)

[2] Layer a marked orange plaid 2⅜" square atop an orange print 2⅜" square. Sew pair together with two seams, stitching ¼" on each side of drawn line (**Diagram 1**).

[3] Cut apart pair on drawn line to make two triangle units (**Diagram 2**). Press open each triangle unit, pressing seam toward orange plaid triangle, to make two triangle-squares (**Diagram 3**). Each triangle-square should be 2" square including seam allowances.

[4] Repeat steps 2 and 3 to make 40 triangle-squares total.

assemble bag front and back

[1] Referring to **Diagram 4**, lay out a multicolor dot 2×12½" rectangle, 20 triangle-squares, and 20 blue floral 2" squares in six horizontal rows.

[2] Sew together pieces in each row. Press seams toward triangle-squares. Join rows to make bag front; press seams in one direction.

[3] Repeat steps 1 and 2 to make bag back.

assemble outer bag

[1] Layer bag front with batting and muslin 9½×12½" rectangles. (For details, see Complete the Quilt, *page 158*.) Baste layers a scant ¼" from all edges. Quilt as desired. (The featured bag is machine-quilted with an allover stipple.) Repeat with bag back.

[2] Layer multicolor dot 3½×9½" rectangle with batting and muslin 3½×9½" rectangles. Baste layers a scant ¼" from all edges to make the bag base. Quilt as desired.

[3] Mark center bottom of bag front and back. Mark center of each long edge of the bag base (**Diagram 5**).

[4] Matching centers, sew bag base to bag front and back (**Diagram 6**). Press seams toward bag base. Topstitch bag base through all layers, about ⅛" from seams.

[5] Fold a blue floral 2×18½" strip in half lengthwise with right side inside; stitch along long edges. Trim seam to ⅛" and turn right side out. Press flat and topstitch ⅛" from long edges to make a handle. Repeat to make a second handle.

[6] Pin handles to top of bag front and back with ends about 2¼" from side edges; baste (**Diagram 7**).

[7] Sew bag front to bag back along sides; press seams open. Mark center of each short edge of bag base with a pin. Fold bag so one pin matches corresponding side seam (**Diagram 8**). Stitch across end of bag. Repeat with other side of bag to complete outer bag.

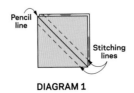

DIAGRAM 1

DIAGRAM 2

DIAGRAM 3

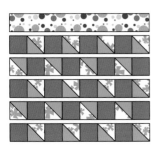

DIAGRAM 4

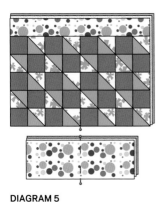

DIAGRAM 5

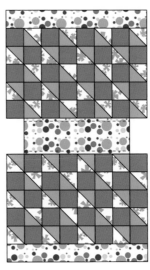

DIAGRAM 6

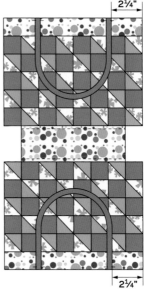

DIAGRAM 7

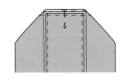

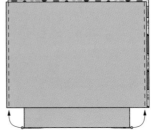

DIAGRAM 8

assemble lining

[1] Mark center bottom of blue floral 9½×12½" rectangles. Mark center of each long edge of blue floral 3½×9½" rectangle. Matching centers, sew large rectangles to small rectangle to make lining; press seams toward small rectangle. Topstitch small rectangle about ⅛" from the seams.

[2] Sew together sides of bag lining, leaving a 5" opening for turning on one side. Press seams open. Mark center of each short edge of the lining base with a pin. Referring to **Diagram 8**, fold lining so one pin matches the corresponding side seam. Stitch across end of lining. Repeat with other side of lining.

finish bag

[1] Place lining inside outer bag with right sides together and side seams matching. Stitch along top edges. Turn bag right side out through opening in the lining. Slip-stitch opening closed. Smooth lining inside bag. Press bag's upper edge and topstitch ⅛" from edge.

[2] For a sturdier bag, place cardboard 3×9" rectangle in bottom of bag.

wild at heart

You'll be ever-so-popular when you make and give this softest-ever, no-batting throw.

DESIGNERS **MELANIE GRESETH AND JOANIE HOLTON**
PHOTOGRAPHER **ANDY LYONS**

materials

- ⅞ yard green zebra print (blocks, binding)
- 1 ⅛ yards green polka dot (blocks, backing border)
- ½ yard blue cheetah print (blocks)
- ⅞ yard blue polka dot (blocks)
- ½ yard blue zebra print (blocks)
- 1 yard blue floral (backing)

Finished quilt: 42×60"   Finished block: 16½×17"

Quantities are for 60"-wide plush knit-backed fleece fabric.
Measurements include ½" seam allowances unless otherwise stated. Sew with right sides together unless otherwise stated.

fabric notes

Stitching the plush knit-backed fleece fabric (our project uses Minkee Tween from Benartex) is easy; see our tips for working with this specialty fabric on *page 23*.

cut fabrics

Cut pieces in the following order.

From green zebra print, cut:
- 4—2½×56" binding strips
- 2—14×17½" rectangles

From green polka dot, cut:
- 2—6×50" quilt back border strips
- 2—6×42" quilt back border strips
- 4—5×17½" rectangles

From blue cheetah print, cut:
- 2—14×17½" rectangles

From blue polka dot, cut:
- 2—5×52" quilt top border strips
- 2—5×42" quilt top border strips
- 2—5×17½" rectangles

From blue zebra print, cut:
- 2—14×17½" rectangles

From blue floral, cut:
- 1—32×50" quilt back rectangle

assemble blocks

[1] Referring to **Block Assembly Diagram** for placement, sew together a green zebra print 14×17½" rectangle and a green polka dot 5×17½" rectangle to make a green block. Finger-press seam toward larger rectangle. The block should be 17½×18" including seam allowances. Repeat to make a second green block.

[2] Using a blue cheetah print 14×17½" rectangle and a blue polka dot 5×17½" rectangle, repeat Step 1 to make a blue cheetah block.

[3] Using a blue zebra print 14×17½" rectangle and a green polka dot 5×17½" rectangle, repeat Step 1 to make a blue-zebra-and-green block.

[4] Using a blue cheetah print 14×17½" rectangle and a green polka dot 5×17½" rectangle, repeat Step 1 to make a blue-cheetah-and-green block.

[5] Using a blue zebra print 14×17½" rectangle and a blue polka dot 5×17½" rectangle, repeat Step 1 to make a blue zebra block.

assemble quilt top

[1] Referring to **Quilt Assembly Diagram**, sew together blocks in two vertical rows. Finger-press seams in one

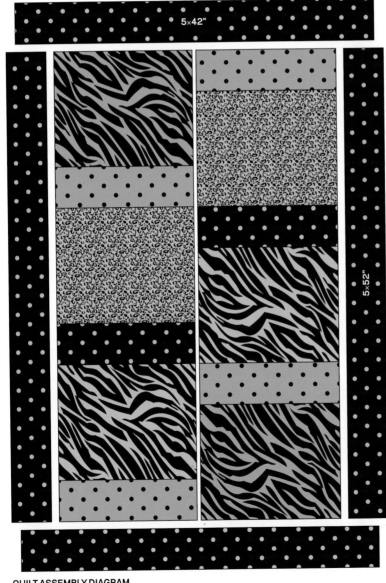

QUILT ASSEMBLY DIAGRAM

BLOCK ASSEMBLY DIAGRAM

6×42"

32×50"

6×50"

QUILT BACK ASSEMBLY DIAGRAM

assemble quilt back

Referring to **Quilt Back Assembly Diagram**, sew long green polka dot border strips to long edges of blue floral quilt back rectangle. Add remaining green polka dot border strips to remaining edges to complete quilt back. Finger-press all seams toward border.

finish quilt

[1] Layer quilt top and back, matching outer corners of quilt top to outer corners of quilt back. Baste. (For details, see Complete the Quilt, *page 158.*)

[2] Quilt as desired, using a walking foot on your machine. This quilt features outline-quilting around the rectangles in each block 2¼" from each seam.

[3] Bind with green zebra print binding strips. (For details, see Better Binding, *page 159.*)

tip

Make this project in favorite cotton prints. Add lightweight batting and machine-quilt with an overall motif for a fast-to-sew gift.

direction, alternating direction with each row.

[2] Join rows to make quilt center. Finger-press seam in one direction. The quilt center should be 34×52" including seam allowances.

[3] Sew long blue polka dot border strips to long edges of quilt center. Add remaining blue polka dot border strips to remaining edges to complete quilt top. Finger-press all seams toward border.

it's a hoot

You can't help but smile at this adorably sweet pillow easily made with fusible appliqué, embroidery, and rickrack.

DESIGNER **JENNIFER DAVIS**   PHOTOGRAPHER **ADAM ALBRIGHT**

materials

- 7×9" rectangle solid cream (block background)
- 6×10" rectangle brown print (appliqué)
- Scraps of blue dot, solid light green, and light green dot (appliqués)
- Scrap of white felted wool (appliqués)
- Coral dot (border, pillow back)
- Embroidery floss: light blue
- 2—¼"-diameter buttons: black
- 45"-long jumbo (⅝"-wide) rickrack: blue
- Lightweight fusible web (see Tip, *page 98*)
- Polyester fiberfill
- Water-soluble marking pen
- Chopstick

Finished pillow: 9×11"   Finished block: 7×9"

Quantities are for 44/45"-wide, 100% cotton fabrics unless otherwise specified.
Measurements include ½" seam allowances. Sew with right sides together unless otherwise stated.

cut fabrics

Cut pieces in the following order. Patterns A–G and Full-Size Embroidery Pattern are on *Pattern Sheet 2*.

To use fusible web for appliquéing, complete the following steps.

[1] Lay fusible web, paper side up, over patterns A–G. Use a pencil to trace each pattern the number of times indicated in cutting instructions, leaving ½" between tracings. Cut out each fusible-web shape roughly ¼" outside traced lines.

APPLIQUÉ PLACEMENT DIAGRAM

BACKSTITCH

DIAGRAM 1

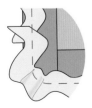

DIAGRAM 2

[2] Following the manufacturer's instructions, press fusible-web shapes onto wrong sides of designated fabrics; let cool. Cut out fabric shapes on drawn lines. Peel off paper backings.

From brown print, cut:
▸ 1 of Pattern A
From blue dot, cut:
▸ 1 of Pattern B
From solid light green, cut:
▸ 1 each of patterns C, D, and E
From light green dot, cut:
▸ 11 of Pattern G
From white wool, cut:
▸ 2 of Pattern F
From coral dot, cut:
▸ 1—10×12" rectangle
▸ 2—2×12" long border strips
▸ 2—2×7" short border strips

tip

If you don't want to stitch inside the edges of the appliqués, choose heavyweight fusible web rather than lightweight. It allows for a stronger bond of fabric to the pillow top.

appliqué and assemble pillow top

[1] Referring to Appliqué Placement Diagram, place A–G pieces on solid cream 7×9" rectangle. Fuse in place.

[2] Using coordinating threads and a short stitch length, machine-straight-stitch $\frac{1}{16}$" to $\frac{1}{8}$" inside edges of each appliqué. Stitch again over first stitching to make appliquéd block.

[3] Sew coral dot short border strips to short edges of appliquéd block. Add coral dot long border strips to remaining edges to make pillow top. Press all seams toward border.

embellish pillow top

[1] Referring to photo, *opposite*, and using a light box or window and a water-soluble marking pen, trace Embroidery Pattern onto pillow top.

[2] Using two strands of light blue floss, backstitch words onto pillow top.

To backstitch, pull needle up at A (**Backstitch Diagram**). Insert it back into fabric at B and bring it up at C. Push needle down again at D and bring it up at E. Continue in same manner.

[3] Referring to photo, center a black button over each white wool F circle and attach with black thread.

finish pillow

[1] Leaving a 2" tail, pin center of rickrack ½" from edge of pillow top, easing rickrack around corners (**Diagram 1**).

[2] Tuck raw ends of rickrack into seam allowance so raw edges will be sewn into seam later (**Diagram 2**).

[3] Machine-baste rickrack to pillow top using a scant ½" seam. Remove each pin just before the needle reaches it.

[4] With right sides together, pin pillow top to coral dot 10×12" pillow back.

[5] Using a ½" seam, sew together around all edges, leaving a 3" opening for turning.

[6] Turn pillow right side out. Using a chopstick, stuff firmly with fiberfill, being sure to poke fiberfill into all four corners.

[7] Slip-stitch opening closed to complete pillow.

cozy up

Get in the swim of things year-round
by making a colorful, big-block quilt that will
add a splash of style to your bedroom.

DESIGNER **MARK LIPINSKI**   QUILTMAKER **JUDY SOHN**   QUILTER **NANCY SHARR**
PHOTOGRAPHER **ANDY LYONS AND MARTY BALDWIN**

materials

- 1⅛ yards green leaf flannel (quilt center)
- 1½ yards mottled green flannel (quilt center)
- ¼ yard each dark brown, medium brown, and light brown flannel (quilt center)
- 2⅛ yards green pinecone flannel (quilt center, outer border)
- 1⅛ yards mottled blue flannel (quilt center, outer border)
- 1½ yards brown print flannel (inner border, binding)
- ½ yard brown plaid flannel (outer border)
- ⅞ yard green plaid flannel (outer border)
- 5⅓ yards backing fabric
- 83×95" batting

Finished quilt: 76½×88½"

Quantities are for 44/45"-wide, 100% cotton fabrics.
Measurements include a ¼" seam allowance. Sew with right sides together unless otherwise stated.

cut fabrics

To make the best use of your fabrics, cut pieces in the following order. Cut mottled green flannel strip and green pinecone flannel strips lengthwise (parallel to the selvage).

From green leaf flannel, cut:
- 1—6½x24½" rectangle
- 2—12½" squares
- 3—6½x12½" rectangles
- 1—6⅞" square, cutting it in half diagonally for 2 triangles total
- 6—6½" squares

From mottled green flannel, cut:
- 1—6½x42½" strip
- 1—6½x18½" rectangle
- 1—12½" square
- 1—6½x12½" rectangle
- 6—6½" squares
- 13—6⅞" squares, cutting each in half diagonally for 26 triangles total

From dark brown flannel, cut:
- 4—6⅞" squares, cutting each in half diagonally for 8 triangles total

From medium brown flannel, cut:
- 4—6⅞" squares, cutting each in half diagonally for 8 triangles total

From light brown flannel, cut:
- 4—6⅞" squares, cutting each in half diagonally for 8 triangles total

From green pinecone flannel, cut:
- 1—6½x48½" strip
- 1—6½x36½" strip
- 4—12½" squares
- 16—6½" squares

From mottled blue flannel, cut:
- 4—12½" squares
- 4—6½x12" rectangles
- 2—6½" squares

From brown print flannel, cut:
- 8—2½x42" strips for inner border
- 1—30" square, cutting it into enough 2½"-wide bias strips to total 350" for binding (For details, see Cutting on the Bias, *page 158*.)

From brown plaid flannel, cut:
- 4—6½x15" rectangles

From green plaid flannel, cut:
- 4—6½x15" rectangles
- 4—6½x12" rectangles

assemble triangle-squares

[1] Sew together a green leaf flannel triangle and a mottled green flannel triangle to make a print triangle-square (**Diagram 1**). Press seam toward mottled green flannel. The triangle-square should be 6½" square including seam allowances. Repeat to make a second print triangle-square.

[2] Repeat Step 1 using mottled dark brown, medium brown, and light brown flannel triangles in place of the green leaf flannel triangles to make eight dark brown triangle-squares, eight medium brown triangle-squares, and eight light brown triangle-squares total.

assemble four-patch units

Sew together two green leaf flannel 6½" squares and two mottled green flannel 6½" squares in pairs. Press seams in opposite directions. Join pairs to make a Four-Patch unit (**Diagram 2**). Press seam in one direction. The unit should be 12½" square including seam allowances. Repeat to make three Four-Patch units total.

assemble upper section

Assemble this quilt in two sections. For specific pieces to use, see **Quilt Assembly Diagram**.

[1] Lay out pieces in Row 1; sew together. Press seams toward mottled green flannel triangle-square.

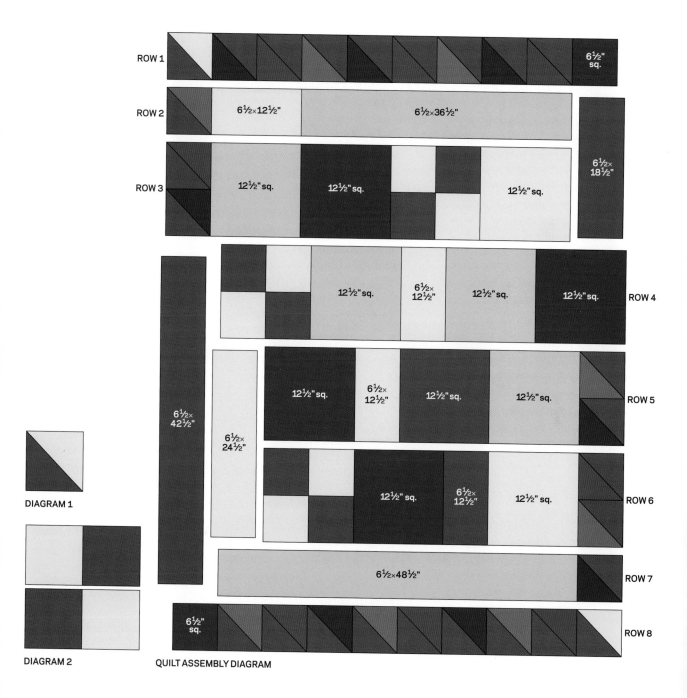

ROW 1

ROW 2 — 6½×12½" 6½×36½"

ROW 3 — 12½" sq. 12½" sq. 12½" sq.

6½"
sq.

6½×
18½"

12½" sq. 6½×
12½" 12½" sq. 12½" sq. — ROW 4

DIAGRAM 1

6½×
42½"

6½×
24½"

12½" sq. 6½×
12½" 12½" sq. 12½" sq. — ROW 5

12½" sq. 6½×
12½" 12½" sq. — ROW 6

6½×48½" — ROW 7

DIAGRAM 2

6½"
sq.

ROW 8

QUILT ASSEMBLY DIAGRAM

[2] Lay out pieces in Row 2; sew together. Press seams toward green pinecone flannel rectangle.

[3] Sew together a medium brown triangle-square and a dark brown triangle-square to make a triangle-square unit. Lay out triangle-square unit and other pieces in Row 3; sew together. Press seams toward triangle-square unit.

[4] Join rows 2 and 3; press seam in one direction. Add mottled green flannel 6½×18½" rectangle to right-hand edge of joined rows; press seam toward just-added rectangle. Add Row 1 to top edge of joined rows to make upper section.

tip

For a big-block quilt like this one, auditioning fabric combinations can be tough . To experiment before you cut into your fabric, make color photocopies of the fabrics and arrange paper pieces first.

assemble lower section

For specific pieces to use, see **Quilt Assembly Diagram**, *page 103*.

[1] Lay out pieces in Row 4; sew together. Press seams toward mottled blue flannel.

[2] Join a light brown triangle-square and dark brown triangle-square as before to make a triangle-square unit. Lay out triangle-square unit and other pieces in Row 5; sew together. Press seams toward mottled blue flannel.

[3] Join a medium brown triangle-square and light brown triangle-square as before to make a triangle-square unit. Lay out triangle-square unit and other pieces in Row 6; sew together. Press seams toward triangle-square unit.

[4] Lay out pieces in Row 7; sew together. Press seams toward green pinecone flannel.

[5] Lay out pieces in Row 8; sew together. Press seams toward mottled green flannel.

[6] Join rows 5 and 6; press seam in one direction. Add green leaf flannel 6½×24½" rectangle to left-hand edge of joined rows; press seam toward just-added rectangle.

[7] Join rows 4, 5, 6, and 7; press seams in one direction. Add mottled green flannel 6½×42½" strip to left-hand edge of joined rows; press seam toward just-added rectangle. Add Row 8 to the bottom edge to complete the lower section.

assemble quilt top

[1] Join upper and lower sections to make quilt center. Press seam in one direction. The quilt center should be 60½×72½" including seam allowances.

[2] Cut and piece brown print 2½×42" strips to make:
  ‣ 2—2½×80" inner border strips
  ‣ 2—2½×68" inner border strips

[3] Beginning and ending ¼" from quilt center edges, sew short inner border strips to short edges of quilt center. Repeat to add long inner border strips to

make top outer border strip. Repeat to make bottom outer border strip.

[6] Sew side outer border strips to side edges of quilt center. Add top and bottom outer border strips to remaining quilt center edges to complete quilt top. Press seams toward outer border.

finish quilt

[1] Layer quilt top, batting, and backing; baste. (For details, see Complete the Quilt, *page 158.*)

[2] Quilt as desired.

[3] Bind with brown print flannel binding strips. (For details, see Better Binding, *page 159.*)

remaining quilt center edges, mitering the corners. (For details, see Mitering Borders, *page 157.*) Press all seams toward inner border.

[4] Referring to photograph *above*, sew together three green pinecone flannel 6½" squares, two brown plaid flannel 6½×15" rectangles, and two green plaid flannel

6½×15" rectangles to make a side outer border strip. Press seams in one direction. Repeat to make a second side outer border strip.

[5] Join five green pinecone flannel 6½" squares, two mottled blue flannel 6½×12" rectangles, and two green plaid flannel 6½×12" rectangles to

grab&go

The simple backpack uses a double drawstring closure so kids can keep their treasures safe yet accessible.

DESIGNERS **WEEKS RINGLE AND BILL KERR**   PHOTOGRAPHER **GREG SCHEIDEMANN**

materials

- ½ yard each of solid blue (bag body) and black-and-white print (bag lining)
- 6—3×8" pieces assorted novelty prints (pocket)
- ¼ yard black-and-white stripe (straps/drawstring)
- 18×33" batting
- Jeans needle

for optional name tag:
- Scrap of solid white (front)
- 3½×8" piece red-and-orange dot (border, back)
- Scrap of iron-on, heavy-duty interfacing (such as Fast2Fuse)
- Permanent fabric pen

Finished bag: 11½×16"

Quantities are for 44/45"-wide, 100% cotton fabrics. Measurements include ¼" seam allowances. Sew with right sides together unless otherwise stated.

choose your fabrics

This bag uses a solid navy blue for the main fabric because it hides stains and looks good in both summer and winter. A stripe fabric creates a fun strap or drawstring when cut perpendicular to the stripe.

For the novelty print pockets, select fabrics appropriate to the scale of the pieces used. To fussy-cut six 2½×7" rectangles for the pockets, see Fussy-Cutting Fabrics on *page 111*.

cut fabrics

Cut pieces in the following order.

From solid blue, cut:
- 2—13×17" rectangles
- 1—7×13" rectangle
- 2—3×12½" rectangles

From black-and-white print, cut:
- 2—13×17" lining rectangles

From assorted novelty prints, cut:
- 6—2½×7" rectangles

From black-and-white stripe, cut:
- 3 to 4—2×42" strips (For a child under 50" tall, use 3 strips; for a taller child, cut 4 strips.)

From batting, cut:
- 2—12¾×16¾" rectangles
- 1—6¾×12¾" rectangle

For optional name tag:
From solid white, cut:
- 1—2×3" rectangle

From red-and-orange dot, cut:
- 1—3×4" rectangle
- 4—1×3" strips

From iron-on, heavy-duty interfacing, cut:
- 1—2¼×3¼" rectangle

assemble backpack panels

[1] With right sides together, layer a solid blue 13×17" rectangle and a black-and-white print 13×17" rectangle. Center 12¾×16¾" batting rectangle on top; pin all layers together. Sew around three sides, leaving one short edge (the bottom) open. Turn right side out; press.

[2] Turn raw edges of Step 1 unit ¼" to wrong side. Machine-stitch ⅛" from edges to close opening and make a bag panel. Quilt bag panel as desired. This version features machine-quilt parallel lines ¾" apart (**Diagram 1**).

[3] Repeat steps 1 and 2 to make a second bag panel.

assemble pocket panel

[1] Referring to **Diagram 2**, sew together six assorted novelty print 2½×7" rectangles along long edges to make a pocket rectangle. Press seams open to reduce bulk.

[2] With right sides together, layer pocket rectangle and solid blue 7×13" rectangle. Center 6¾×12¾" batting rectangle on top; pin all layers together. Sew around three sides, leaving one long edge (the bottom) open, to create pocket panel. Turn right side out; press.

[3] Quilt pocket panel as desired. The version shown was machine-quilted with an allover stipple.

[4] Topstitch ⅛" from top edge of panel for added durability.

make straps/ drawstrings

Piece black-and-white stripe 2×42" strips to make one long strip. Fold strip in half lengthwise with wrong side inside; press. Open up strip, then turn in raw edges to meet at center fold line (**Diagram 3**). Refold along center fold line and press. Stitch ⅛" away from long, double-fold edge.

DIAGRAM 1

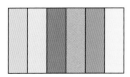

DIAGRAM 2

DIAGRAM 3

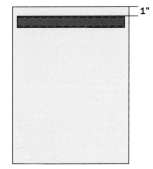

1"

DIAGRAM 4

red-and-orange dot 1×3" strips to remaining edges to make name tag front as shown in photo, opposite. Press all seams toward strips.

[3] With right sides together, layer name tag front and red-and-orange dot 3×4" rectangle; pin together. Sew around three sides, leaving one short edge open (the side that will be attached to the name tag strap). Turn right side out; press.

[4] Slip 2¼×3¼" interfacing rectangle inside name tag. Tuck raw edges of open end under interfacing; insert 6"-long strap about ½", then press to fuse all layers together. Using jeans needle, topstitch ⅛" from edges and ⅛" from seam between solid white and red-and-orange dot to make name tag.

Cut prepared strip into two straps/drawstrings of equal lengths. (Optional: Cut a 6"-long name tag strap from prepared strip; set aside. Cut remaining prepared strip into two straps/drawstrings.)

assemble and add casings

[1] Fold a solid blue 3×12½" rectangle in half lengthwise with right side inside. Sew along long edges and turn right side out. Tuck raw ends ¼" to the inside; press. Topstitch ends closed to make a casing rectangle. Repeat to make a second casing rectangle.

[2] Position a casing rectangle on lining side of each bag panel with casing top edge 1" from top of bag panel and casing centered across panel width. Sew through all layers ⅛" from each long edge of casing rectangle, backstitching at each end of stitching for added durability (**Diagram 4**).

assemble name tag (optional)

[1] Using a permanent fabric pen, write child's name in center of solid white 2×3" rectangle.

[2] Sew red-and-orange dot 1×3" strips to long edges of solid white rectangle. Add

tip

When assembling quilted bags, use a jeans needle (size 100/16 jeans/denim) to easily stitch through multiple layers.

finish backpack

[1] Fasten a safety pin to end of one strap/drawstring. Insert safety pin through casing on one backpack panel, then pull strap/drawstring through. Repeat to run the same strap/drawstring through casing on remaining backpack panel (see red strap on **Diagram 5**). Make sure that the strap does not twist inside casing. Starting from opposite edge, repeat to run remaining strap/drawstring through casings in opposite direction (see green strap on **Diagram 5**).

[2] Pin ends of first strap/drawstring to one side of a backpack panel, 1½" from bottom edge (this will be the front backpack panel). Repeat to pin ends of second strap/drawstring to remaining side of front backpack panel. Draw up drawstring to close top of backpack panels. Have the child try on the backpack panels; adjust strap/drawstring length if necessary, allowing extra length for bulky clothing.

[3] With right sides together, position pocket panel upside down on front backpack panel so bottoms of each overlap by 1" (**Diagram 6**).

[4] Using a jeans needle for this step and those that follow, machine-stitch ⅛" from bottom edge of pocket panel. (Optional: Pin end of name tag strap to side edge of front backpack panel, about 6" from bottom edge of panel.)

[5] Flip pocket panel up along stitching and pin side edges to front backpack panel. Topstitch a vertical line through center of pocket panel to create two smaller pockets, backstitching to secure seam ends.

[6] Layer front and back backpack panels with right sides together. Beginning and ending ½" below casing rectangles, sew panels together along sides and bottom edge to complete backpack. Be careful not to catch middle of strap in stitching.

[7] To box bottom corners of backpack, align bottom seam with side seam at each corner to make a triangle. Sew across triangle several times, about 1" from point (**Diagram 7**). The seam will be bulky, so gently ease backpack through the machine. Trim excess fabric. Turn bag right side out.

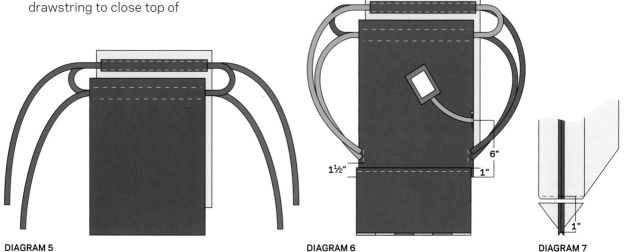

DIAGRAM 5

1½"

6"

1"

1"

DIAGRAM 6

DIAGRAM 7

fussy-cutting fabrics

Isolating and cutting out a specific pattern or print is referred to as "fussy-cutting." Learn these tips for using this technique, then try fussy-cutting the pocket rectangles for your version of "Grab & Go."

When you want to cut an exact part of a print, pattern, or shape, follow these steps for easy fussy-cutting.

use a viewing window

Prevent surprises by using a viewing window to help you fussy-cut any shape:

1. Trace finished-size shape on a piece of frosted template plastic that is at least 2" larger on all sides than desired shape (**Photo A**).
2. Using a crafts knife and ruler, cut away the interior of the shape to make a viewing window (**Photo B**).
3. Move the viewing window over the fabric to isolate the desired portion of the print (**Photo C**). Mark position with pins or chalk.
4. Remove viewing window and re-mark as needed. Add seam allowances and cut out the print portion with scissors or a rotary cutter and ruler.

keep in mind...

For a quicker alternative, use tracing paper to position the piece you want to cut. Trace or photocopy both the finished-size and seam lines on multiple sheets of tracing paper. Lay a marked sheet of tracing paper on the fabric, placing the desired area within the seam lines. Using a rotary cutter and acrylic ruler, cut through all layers at once.

You also can purchase acrylic rulers and templates made just for fussy-cutting common shapes. Or, for squares or rectangles, block off the portion you need with painter's tape or vinyl-cling material.

Fussy-cutting almost always requires more yardage.

Because you align shapes with a fabric's print instead of its selvages, fussy-cut pieces often aren't on grain. Starch fabric to stabilize it for cutting and stitching.

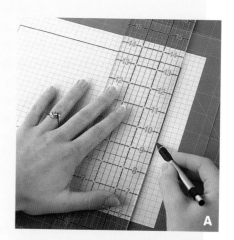

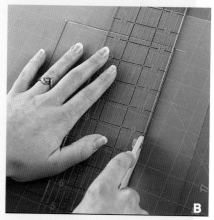

storybook *surprise*

Novelty fabrics star in this lively asymmetrical quilt made from easily pieced chunks of fabric.

DESIGNER **AMY SCHIMLER**   QUILTMAKER **MARY PEPPER**
PHOTOGRAPHER **CAMERON SADEGHPOUR**

materials

- ¼ yard pink print (house unit, inner border)
- 5×10" rectangle multicolor dot (house unit)
- ¾ yard multicolor stripe (house unit, outer border, binding)
- ¼ yard leaf print (forest unit, middle border)
- 5×10" rectangle owl print (forest unit)
- ¼ yard yellow print (quilt center)
- ¼ yard snail print (quilt center)
- 5×10" rectangle bird print (outer border)
- ⅞ yard backing fabric
- 31" square batting

Finished quilt: 24½" square

Quantities are for 44/45"-wide, 100% cotton fabrics. Measurements include ¼" seam allowances. Sew with right sides together unless otherwise stated.

cut fabrics

Cut pieces in the following order. Patterns are on *Pattern Sheet 3*. To make and use templates, see Make and Use Templates on *page 154*.

From pink print, cut:
- 1—2½×18½" inner border strip
- 1—2½×16½" inner border strip
- 2—2×5½" rectangles
- 1 each of patterns A and A reversed

From multicolor dot, cut:
- 1 of Pattern B

From multicolor stripe, cut:
- 1—5½" square
- Enough 2½"-wide bias strips to total 120" for binding (For details, see Cutting on the Bias on *page 158*.)

- ▸ 3—2½×22½" outer border strips
- ▸ 1—2½×12½" outer border strip
- ▸ 1—2½×4½" outer border strip

From leaf print, cut:
- ▸ 1—2½×20½" middle border strip
- ▸ 1—2½×18½" middle border strip
- ▸ 1—6½×8½" rectangle

From owl print, cut:
- ▸ 1—2½×8½" rectangle

From yellow print, cut:
- ▸ 1—4½×16½" rectangle

From snail print, cut:
- ▸ 1—4½×16½" rectangle

From bird print, cut:
- ▸ 1—2½×6½" rectangle

assemble quilt center

[1] With bottom edges aligned, sew pink print A reversed triangle to one short edge of multicolor dot B triangle (**Diagram 1**). Press seam toward multicolor dot triangle.

[2] Add pink print A triangle to remaining short edge of multicolor dot B triangle to make roof unit. Press seam toward pink triangle. The roof unit should be 3½×8½" including seam allowances.

[3] Sew pink print 2×5½" rectangles to opposite edges of multicolor stripe 5½" square to make base unit (**Diagram 2**). Press seams toward square. The base unit should be 5½×8½" including seam allowances.

[4] Join roof unit to base unit to make house unit. Press seam toward base unit.

[5] Referring to **Diagram 3**, join leaf print 6½×8½" rectangle to bottom edge of owl print 2½×8½" rectangle to make forest unit. Press seam toward owl print rectangle.

[6] Join house unit and forest unit. Press seam toward forest unit. Sew yellow print 4½×16½" rectangle to top edge and snail print 4½×16½" rectangle to bottom edge. Press seams toward rectangles to make quilt center. The quilt center should be 16½" square including seam allowances.

tip

Pay attention to the direction of the motifs on the fabric when you plan your cutting so prints such as animals, don't end up upside down when pieced.

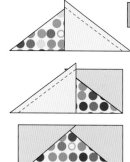

DIAGRAM 1

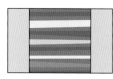

DIAGRAM 2

DIAGRAM 3

add borders

[1] Sew short pink print inner border strip to left edge of quilt center. Add long pink print inner border strip to top edge. Press all seams toward border.

[2] Join short leaf print middle border strip to left edge of quilt center. Add long leaf print middle border strip to top edge. Press all seams toward middle border.

[3] Join multicolor stripe 2½×22½" outer border strip to top edge of quilt center, sewing only half of the seam (Diagram 3). Finger-press seam toward outer border.

[4] Add remaining multicolor stripe 2½×22½" outer border strips clockwise around quilt center. Press all seams toward outer border.

[5] Join a short edge of multicolor stripe 2½×4½" outer border strip to top short edge of bird print 2½×6½" rectangle. Sew short edge of multicolor stripe 2½×12½" outer border strip to remaining short edge of bird print rectangle to make pieced border strip. Press seams toward bird print. The pieced border strip should be 2½×22½" including seam allowances. Join

pieced border strip to remaining edge of quilt center (Diagram 4).

[6] Pin and sew remaining half of top outer border strip to complete quilt top (Diagram 5). Press seam toward outer border.

finish quilt

[1] Layer quilt top, batting, and backing; baste. (For details, see Complete the Quilt, *page 158*.) Quilt as desired.

[2] Bind with multicolor stripe bias binding strips. (For details, see Better Binding, *page 159*.)

DIAGRAM 4

DIAGRAM 5

frill seeking

Cook up some fun in the sewing room before heading to the kitchen with mother-daughter aprons.

DESIGNER **CINDY TAYLOR OATES** PHOTOGRAPHER **ADAM ALBRIGHT**

materials for child-size apron

- ▸ ⅝ yard multicolor stripe (waistband, ties, ruffle)
- ▸ ½ yard pink large floral (apron tier, yo-yo)
- ▸ ¼ yard pink medium floral (apron tier, covered button)
- ▸ ⅛ yard green print (apron tier, leaves)
- ▸ ¾"-diameter (size 30) button to cover or button with a shank

materials for adult-size apron

- ▸ ⅝ yard multicolor stripe (waistband, ties, ruffle)
- ▸ ½ yard pink large floral (apron tier, yo-yo)
- ▸ ¼ yard pink medium floral (apron tier, covered button)
- ▸ ¼ yard green print (apron tier, leaves)
- ▸ ¾"-diameter (size 30) button to cover or button with a shank

Finished apron:
child-size: width at waistband, 20"; length, 14½"
adult-size: width at waistband, 23½"; length, 19¼"

Quantities are for 44/45"-wide, 100% cotton fabrics.
Measurements include ½" seam allowances. Sew with right sides together unless otherwise stated.

cut fabrics for child-size apron

Cut pieces in the following order. Circle Pattern is on *Pattern Sheet 1*.

From multicolor stripe, cut:
- ▸ 1—2¾×42" strip
- ▸ 1—2¾×34" strip
- ▸ 2—4×24" strips
- ▸ 1—3½×21" strip

From pink large floral, cut:
- ▸ 1—6×42" strip
- ▸ 1—6×12" strip
- ▸ 1 of Circle Pattern

From pink medium floral, cut:
- ▸ 1—5×38" strip
- ▸ Scrap to cover button

From green print, cut:
- ▸ 1—4×270" strip
- ▸ 2—1½×4½" bias strips (See Cutting on the Bias on *page 158*.)

assemble apron body

[1] Join multicolor stripe 2¾×42" and 2¾×34" strips together along one short edge to make a 2¾×75" ruffle strip. Press seam open.

[2] Turn under ¼" on one long edge of ruffle strip; press. Turn under a second time ½"; press. Sew through all layers close to first folded edge to hem.

[3] With a basting stitch, sew ½" from long raw edge of ruffle strip. Pull up threads to gather edge (see Tip on page 119).

[4] Join pink large floral 6×42" and 6×12" strips together along one short edge to make 6×53" bottom tier strip. Press seam open.

[5] With raw edges aligned, match center of gathered ruffle strip with center of bottom tier strip. Pin and stitch with ½" seam (**Diagram 1**, *page 118*). Finish raw edges of seam with a machine zigzag stitch to prevent fraying. Press seam toward bottom tier.

[6] Repeat Step 3 to gather raw edge of bottom tier.

kids **117**

[7] With raw edges aligned, match center of gathered bottom tier with center of pink medium floral 5×38" middle tier strip. Pin and stitch with ½" seam. Finish seam as before and press toward middle tier.

[8] In the same manner, repeat Step 3 to gather raw edge of middle tier. Repeat Step 5 to join green print 4×27" top tier strip to make apron body.

[9] Repeat Step 2 to hem each apron side.

make ties

[1] With wrong side inside, press a multicolor stripe 4×24" strip in half lengthwise. Sew along long edge and across one short end at an angle (Diagram 2). Clip corners and turn strip to right side; press.

[2] Pleat raw end of strip so strip end is 1¼" wide. Pin in place, then stitch across pleat to complete an apron tie (Diagram 3).

[3] Repeat steps 1 and 2 with remaining multicolor stripe 4×24" strip to make a second apron tie.

make and add waistband

[1] With wrong side inside, press multicolor stripe 3½×21" strip in half lengthwise. Open strip and press under ¼" along one long edge to make waistband.

[2] With a basting stitch, sew ½" from long raw edge of apron. Pull up thread to gather edge. With raw edges aligned, match center of gathered apron body with center of waistband. (Waistband should extend ½" beyond each apron side edge.)

[3] Sew unpressed edge of waistband to upper edge of apron body. Press seam toward waistband.

[4] Position pleated raw end of apron tie on right side of waistband just below fold (Diagram 4). Fold waistband on previous fold with right side inside (Diagram 5). Sew through all layers with ½" seam (seam line should be even with side edges of apron). Turn waistband and tie right side out; press. Repeat to secure second tie.

[5] Pin long pressed edge of waistband to wrong side of apron body; slip-stitch in place. Topstitch waistband close to bottom edge.

assemble and add yo-yo

[1] Following manufacturer's directions, cover button with scrap of pink medium floral.

[2] Cut a 15" to 18" length of thread and tie a knot about 6" from one end. With pink large floral A circle facedown, turn raw edge of circle a scant ¼" toward circle center. Hand-stitch through folded edge with a running stitch,

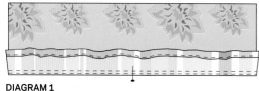

DIAGRAM 1

DIAGRAM 2

DIAGRAM 3

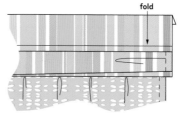

fold

DIAGRAM 4

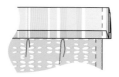

DIAGRAM 5

gathering against the thread knot (**Diagram 6**). Tie thread ends together to make a yo-yo.

[3] Right side inside, fold a green print 1½×4½" bias strip in half lengthwise. Sew along long edge using a ¼" seam. Turn strip to right side. Repeat with remaining bias strip.

[4] Referring to **Diagram 7**, overlap ends of one bias strip; pin and stitch across to make a leaf. Repeat to make a second leaf.

[5] Tuck raw edges of leaves under yo-yo and stitch to apron waistband through all layers. Tack yo-yo to leaves. Sew covered button atop yo-yo to complete apron.

cut fabrics for adult-size apron

From multicolor stripe, cut:
- 1—2¾×42" strip
- 1—2¾×34" strip
- 2—4½×30" strips
- 1—4×24½" strip

From pink large floral, cut:
- 1—7½×42" strip
- 1—7½×14" strip
- 1 of Circle Pattern

From pink medium floral, cut:
- 1—6¼×39" strip
- Scrap to cover button

From green print, cut:
- 1—5¼×28" strip
- 2—1½×4½" bias strips

assemble apron body

[1] Referring to Assemble Apron Body for child-size apron on *page 117*, steps 1 through 3, make ruffle using multicolor stripe 2¾×42" and 2¾×34" strips.

[2] Referring to Assemble Apron Body for child-size apron, steps 4 through 8, make and attach bottom tier using pink large floral 7½×42" and 7½×14" strips; middle tier using pink medium floral 6¼×39" strip; and top tier using green print 5¼×28" strip.

[3] Referring to Assemble Apron Body for child-size apron, Step 2, hem side edges to make apron body.

make ties

Referring to Make Ties for child-size apron, *page 118*, make two ties using multicolor stripe 4½×30" strips. Pleat each tie so strip end is 1¾" wide.

tip

Leave 6" thread tails at beginning and end of gathering stitches. Wrap tails in a figure eight around a pin to secure each end. Gently pull thread in several places, evenly gathering along length of ruffle.

make and add waistband

Referring to Make and Add Waistband for child-size apron, *page 118*, and using multicolor stripe 4×24½" strip, make and add waistband and ties to apron.

assemble and add yo-yo

Referring to Assemble and Add Yo-Yo for child-size apron, make and attach covered button, yo-yo, and leaves.

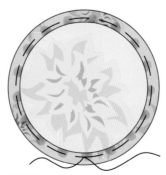

DIAGRAM 6

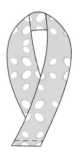

DIAGRAM 7

teens

Appeal to the hip, stylish, and more-grown up tastes of the tween and teenage years with these bold and lively quilts, throws, and pillows that are destined to make a statement.

flower **power**

Attached with fusible web and outlined with machine appliqué, these retro flower blocks are a piece of cake to make.

DESIGNER **KEVIN KOSBAB**   MACHINE QUILTER **JEANETTE LOPES**   PHOTOGRAPHER **CAMERON SADEGHPOUR**

materials

- 8 yards total assorted pink-and-orange prints, stripes, and polka dots, and pink and orange solids (appliqué foundations, appliqués)
- ¼ yard solid white (appliqués)
- ¾ yard pink-and-orange stripe (binding)
- 5 yards backing fabric
- 67×91" batting
- Machine-embroidery threads: pink and orange
- Lightweight fusible web

Finished quilt: 60½×84½"
Finished block: 12" square

Quantities are for 44/45"-wide, 100% cotton fabrics.
Measurements include ¼" seam allowances. Sew with right sides together unless otherwise stated.

tip

To make uniform stitches when doing machine appliqué, work slowly and sew at an even pace. Use a tear-away stabilizer behind appliqués when appliquéing.

cut fabrics

Cut pieces in the following order. For more information, see Tip. Patterns are on *Pattern Sheet 3*. To use fusible web for appliquéing, complete the following steps.

[1] Lay fusible web, paper side up, over patterns. Use a pencil to trace each pattern the number of times indicated in cutting instructions, leaving ½" between tracings. Cut out each fusible-web shape roughly ¼" outside traced lines. To avoid stiff appliqué centers, cut about ⅜" inside traced lines of each piece and discard centers.

[2] Following manufacturer's instructions, press fusible-web shapes onto wrong sides of designated fabrics; let cool. Cut out fabric shapes on drawn lines. Peel off paper backing as you fuse each appliqué piece.

From assorted pink-and-orange prints, stripes, and polka dots, and pink and orange solids, cut:
- 35—12½" squares
- 35 of Pattern A
- 16 each of patterns B, D, and E
- 20 of Pattern C

From solid white, cut:
- 3 of Pattern B
- 2 of Pattern C

From pink-and-orange stripe, cut:
- 8—2½×42" binding strips

appliqué blocks

[1] Fold each assorted print, stripe, polka dot, and solid 12½" square in half vertically and horizontally; finger-press folds to create foundation squares with placement guidelines.

[2] Referring to **Block 1 Diagram**, center B and C circles on an A flower; remove paper backings from B and C pieces only and fuse in place. Set up your machine for a 1-mm-long, 3-mm-wide satin stitch. Using thread in a contrasting color and beginning with the bottom layer, machine-satin-stitch around each circle (you may sew through the backing paper on A at inside points of flower). For details on machine appliqué, see Piece and Appliqué, *page 155.*

[3] Center appliquéd A flower on a foundation square, aligning inner points of petals with placement guidelines (**Block 1 Diagram**); remove paper backing and fuse in place. Using contrasting thread and beginning on an outer curve, machine-satin-stitch around flower to make Block 1. For more information on pivoting outer curves, see Piece and Appliqué. Block 1 should be 12½" square including seam allowances.

[4] Referring to corresponding **Block Diagrams 1–5** and using remaining appliqués A–E, repeat steps 2 and 3 to make:
- 3 total of Block 1
- 7 of Block 2
- 9 of Block 3
- 12 of Block 4
- 4 of Block 5

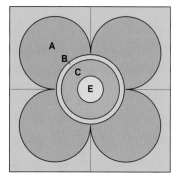

BLOCK 1 DIAGRAM

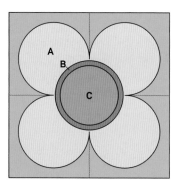

BLOCK 2 DIAGRAM

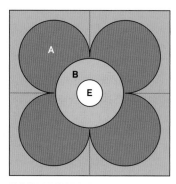

BLOCK 3 DIAGRAM

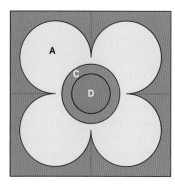

BLOCK 4 DIAGRAM

assemble quilt top

Referring to **Quilt Assembly Diagram**, lay out blocks in seven horizontal rows. Sew together blocks in each row. Press seams in one direction, alternating direction with each row. Join rows to complete quilt top. Press seams in one direction.

finish quilt

[1] Layer quilt top, batting, and backing; baste. (For details, see Complete the Quilt, *page 158*.)

[2] Quilt as desired. This quilt was stitched with meandering lines between the flower appliqués and a small circle in each flower center.

[3] Bind with pink-and-orange stripe binding strips. (For details, see Better Binding, *page 159*.)

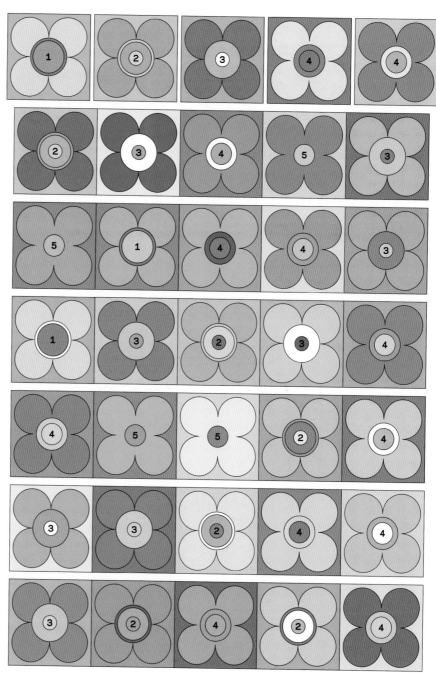

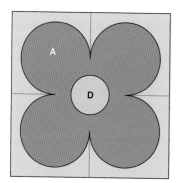

BLOCK 5 DIAGRAM

QUILT ASSEMBLY DIAGRAM

exclamation point

It's a knockout! Machine-appliquéd circles, simple strips, and rectangles make this cozy quilt a snap from start to finish.

DESIGNERS **CORI DERKSEN AND MYRA HARDER**   QUILTMAKER **KATE HARDY**
QUILTER **KAREN GILSON**   PHOTOGRAPHERS **ADAM ALBRIGHT AND MARTY BALDWIN**

materials

- ¾ yard blue swirl batik (appliqués)
- 2½ yards light blue batik (units, inner border)
- ⅜ yard blue dot batik (units)
- 2⅝ yards brown leaf batik (units, outer border)
- ⅜ yard brown diamond batik (units)
- ⅜ yard brown geometric batik (units)
- ⅜ yard brown seed batik (units)
- ⅜ yard blue seed batik (units)
- 3⅛ yards brown batik (sashing)
- 6 yards backing fabric
- 88×112" batting
- Clear monofilament thread
- Template plastic
- Spray starch

Finished quilt: 81½×105½"

Quantities are for 44/45"-wide, 100% cotton fabrics. Measurements include ¼" seam allowances. Sew with right sides together unless otherwise stated.

cut fabrics

To make the best use of your fabrics, cut pieces in the following order. Pattern A is on *Pattern Sheet 2*. To make a template, see Make and Use Templates on *page 154*. Add a scant ½" seam allowance when cutting out fabric circles. Cut sashing and border strips lengthwise (parallel to the selvages).

From blue swirl batik, cut:
- 13 of Pattern A

From light blue batik, cut:
- 2—2½×87½" inner border strips
- 2—2½×67½" inner border strips
- 13—9½" squares
- 16—2×24½" rectangles
- 8—2×15½" rectangles
- 24—2×9½" rectangles

From blue dot batik, cut:
- 2—6½×24½" rectangles

From brown leaf batik, cut:
- 2—7½×91½" outer border strips
- 2—7½×81½" outer border strips
- 2—6½×24½" rectangles

From brown diamond batik, cut:
- 1—6½×24½" rectangle
- 1—6½×15½" rectangle

From brown geometric batik, cut:
- 1—6½×24½" rectangle
- 1—6½×15½" rectangle

From brown seed batik, cut:
- 1—6½×24½" rectangle
- 1—6½×15½" rectangle

From blue seed batik, cut:
- 1—6½×24½" rectangle
- 1—6½×15½" rectangle

From brown batik, cut:
- 6—3½×81½" sashing strips
- 2—3½×63½" sashing strips
- 10—2½×42" binding strips

appliqué unit a

[1] Sew a gathering stitch around a blue dot swirl batik circle ⅛" from the edge. Center Circle Pattern A template on wrong side of circle. Pull gathering thread taut around template (**Diagram 1**). Spray with starch; press to create a finished edge. Let circle cool. Loosen gathering thread just enough to remove template to make circle appliqué.

[2] Center circle appliqué on light blue batik 9½" square (**Appliqué Placement Diagram**). Using clear monofilament thread, blind-hemstitch around appliqué to make a Unit A.

[3] Repeat steps 1 and 2 to make 13 total of Unit A.

assemble units b and c

[1] Sew a light blue batik 2×24½" rectangle to each long edge of a brown seed batik 6½×24½" rectangle (**Diagram 2**). Join a light blue batik 2×9½" rectangle to each short edge to make a Unit B. Press all seams toward brown seed batik rectangle. Unit B should be 9½×27½" including seam allowances.

[2] Repeat Step 1 with remaining light blue batik 2×24½" rectangles, light blue batik 2×9½" rectangles, and remaining dot, leaf, diamond, geometric, and blue seed batik 6½×24½" rectangles to make eight total of Unit B.

[3] Sew a light blue batik 2×15½" rectangle to each long edge of a blue seed batik 6½×15½" rectangle (**Diagram 3**). Join a light blue batik 2×9½" rectangle to each short edge to make a Unit C. Press all seams toward blue seed batik rectangle. Unit C should be 9½×18½" including seam allowances.

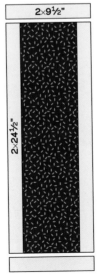

DIAGRAM 1

APPLIQUÉ PLACEMENT DIAGRAM

2×9½"

2×24½"

DIAGRAM 2

2×9½"

2×15½"

DIAGRAM 3

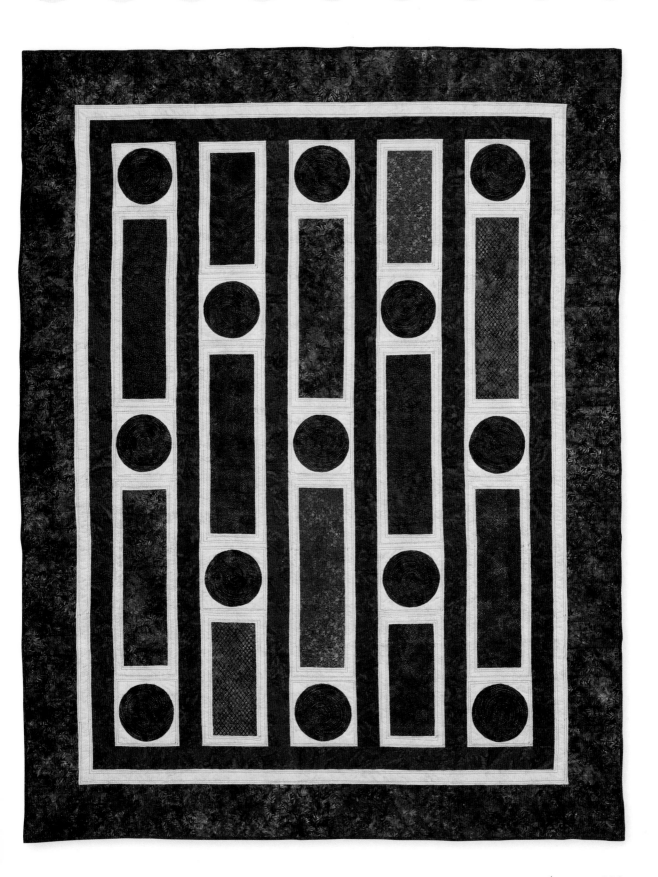

[4] Repeat Step 3 with remaining light blue batik 2×15½" rectangles, light blue batik 2×9½" rectangles, and remaining diamond, geometric, and brown seed batik 6½×15½" rectangles to make four total of Unit C.

assemble rows

[1] Referring to photo on *page 129* and **Quilt Assembly Diagram**, lay out three of Unit A and two of Unit B in a row.

[2] Sew together units; press seams toward A units.

[3] Repeat steps 1 and 2 to make three rows total (rows 1, 3, and 5).

[4] Lay out two of unit A, one of unit B, and two of unit C in a row.

[5] Sew together units; press seams toward A units.

[6] Repeat steps 4 and 5 to make two rows total (rows 2 and 4).

assemble quilt center

[1] Referring to **Quilt Assembly Diagram**, lay out rows 1 through 5, the brown batik 3½×81½" sashing strips, and the brown batik 3½×63½" sashing strips.

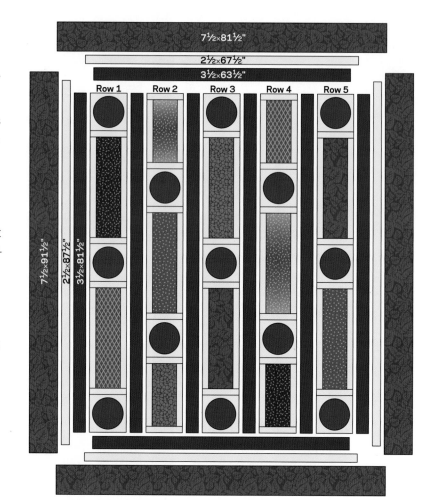

QUILT ASSEMBLY DIAGRAM

[2] Sew together rows and long sashing strips. Join short sashing strips to remaining edges to complete quilt center. Press all seams toward sashing. The quilt center should be 63½×87½" including seam allowances.

add borders

[1] Sew light blue batik 2½×87½" inner border strips to long edges of quilt center. Join light blue batik 2½×67½" inner border strips to remaining edges. Press all seams toward sashing.

[2] Sew brown leaf batik 7½×91½" outer border strips to long edges of quilt center. Join brown leaf batik 7½×81½" border strips to remaining edges to complete quilt top. Press all seams toward outer border.

finish quilt

[1] Layer quilt top, batting, and backing; baste. (For details, see Complete the Quilt, *page 158*.)

[2] Quilt as desired.

[3] Bind with brown batik strips. (For details, see Better Binding, *page 159*.)

materials for the squares pillow

‣ 3—⅛-yard pieces brown-and-blue batiks (blocks)
‣ ½ yard light blue batik (sashing, pillow back)
‣ 12½" square muslin (lining)
‣ 12"-square polyester pillow form

materials for the circles pillow

‣ 6×18" rectangle each brown and blue batik (appliqués)
‣ ¾ yard light blue batik (appliqué foundation, pillow back)
‣ 12½×20½" rectangle muslin (lining)
‣ 12×20" polyester pillow form or polyester fiberfill
‣ Lightweight fusible web

cut and assemble squares pillow

To make the best use of your fabrics, cut pieces in the following order.

From each brown-and-blue batik, cut:
‣ 3—3½" squares
From light blue batik, cut:
‣ 2—12½×16½" rectangles
‣ 4—1¼×12½" sashing strips
‣ 12—1¼×3½" sashing strips

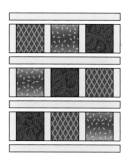

SQUARES PILLOW TOP ASSEMBLY DIAGRAM

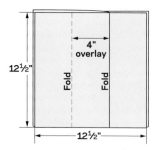

SQUARES PILLOW BACK ASSEMBLY DIAGRAM

[1] Referring to **Squares Pillow Top Assembly Diagram**, lay out nine brown and blue batiks 3½" squares, the light blue batik 1¼×3½" sashing strips, and the light blue batik 1¼×12½" sashing strips.

[2] Sew together pieces in each row. Press seams toward print squares. Join rows and long sashing strips to complete pillow top. Press seams toward sashing strips. Pillow top should be 12½" square including seam allowances.

finish pillow

[1] Layer pillow top and muslin 12½" lining square.

[2] With wrong side inside, fold each light blue batik 12½×16½" rectangle in half to make two 12½×8¼" double-thick pillow back rectangles (**Squares Pillow Back Assembly Diagram**).

[3] Overlap folded edges of pillow back rectangles by about 4" to make a 12½"-square pillow back; baste around outer edges.

[4] Right sides together, join pillow back to quilted pillow top, stitching around all edges, to make pillow cover. Turn right side out and press.

[5] Insert 12"-square pillow form through opening in pillow cover back. If desired, hand-stitch opening closed.

cut circles pillow

To make the best use of your fabrics, cut pieces in the following order. Pattern B is on *Pattern Sheet 2*.

To use fusible web for appliquéing, complete the following steps. (For more information on fusible appliqué, see Piece and Appliqué, *page 155*.)

[1] Lay fusible web, paper side up, over pattern. Use a pencil to trace the pattern six times, leaving ½" between tracings. Cut out each fusible-web shape roughly ¼" outside traced lines.

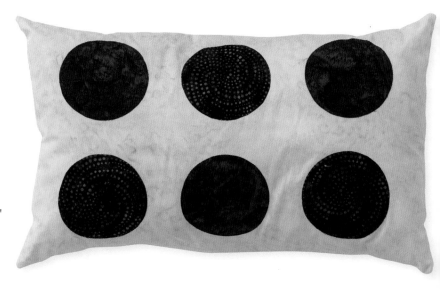

[2] Following manufacturer's instructions, press fusible-web shapes onto backs of designated fabrics; let cool.

[3] Cut out fabric shapes on drawn lines and peel off paper backings.

From each of brown batik and blue batik, cut:
▸ 3 of Pattern B

From light blue batik, cut:
▸ 2—12½×24½" rectangles
▸ 1—12½×20½" rectangle

appliqué pillow top

Referring to **Circles Pillow Top Assembly Diagram**, lay out appliqué circles on light blue batik 12½×20½" rectangle; fuse in place to make pillow top.

finish pillow

[1] Layer pillow top and muslin 12½×20½" lining rectangle. Quilt fused circles with swirl motifs.

[2] With wrong side inside, fold each light blue batik 12½×24½" rectangle in half to make two 12½×12¼" double-thick pillow back rectangles (Circles Pillow Back Assembly Diagram).

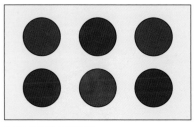

CIRCLES PILLOW TOP
ASSEMBLY DIAGRAM

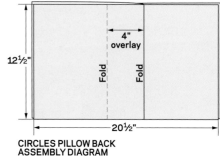

CIRCLES PILLOW BACK
ASSEMBLY DIAGRAM

[3] Overlap folded edges of pillow back rectangles by about 4" to make a 12½×20½" pillow back; baste around outer edges.

[4] Right sides together, join pillow back to pillow top, stitching around all edges, to make pillow cover. Turn right side out and press.

[5] Insert 12×20" pillow form through opening in pillow cover back. (Or stuff pillow with polyester fiberfill.) If desired, hand-stitch opening closed.

tip

Pivoting evenly around appliqué curves takes practice. Keep an eye on the space between your stitches. Pivot often on a gentle curve to maintain evenness between your stitches.

congrats pillow

Celebrate a new graduate's achievement with a simple appliqué pillow that includes a personalized photo transfer panel.

DESIGNER **KAREN MONTGOMERY** PHOTOGRAPHER **MARTY BALDWIN**

materials

- ▸ Inkjet printable sew-on fabric sheet (pillow top center)
- ▸ 9" square solid navy blue (inner border)
- ▸ ¾ yard blue print (outer border, pillow back)
- ▸ 12" square solid yellow (appliqués)
- ▸ 19×16" piece white flannel (pillow top lining)
- ▸ Fusible web
- ▸ White thread
- ▸ 6—¾"-wide balloon-shape buttons: multicolor
- ▸ 16×12" pillow form

Finished pillow: 16×12"

Quantities are for 44/45"-wide, 100% cotton fabrics. Measurements include ¼" seam allowances. Sew with right sides together unless otherwise stated.

cut fabrics

Cut pieces in the following order. Patterns are on *Pattern Sheet 3*.

To use fusible web for appliquéing, complete the following steps.

[1] Lay fusible web, paper side up, over patterns. Use a pencil to trace each pattern once. Cut out fusible-web shape roughly ¼" outside traced lines.

[2] Following manufacturer's instructions, press fusible-web shapes onto back of solid yellow; let cool.

[3] Cut out fabric shapes on drawn lines and peel off paper backing.

From solid navy blue, cut:
▸ 4—1½×7" inner border strips

From blue print, cut:
▸ 2—12½×19½" rectangles
▸ 2—5×15" outer border strips
▸ 1—5½×9" outer border strip
▸ 1—3½×9" outer border strip

From solid yellow, cut:
▸ 1 *each* of patterns C, O, N, G, R, A, T, S, and !

prepare and print photo

[1] On your computer, adjust photo to print at 5×7" (two images will fit on an 8½×11" sheet). Following manufacturer's instructions, print photo onto fabric sheet; let ink dry.

[2] Remove paper backing and trim photo to 5×7" including seam allowances to make pillow top center.

assemble pillow top

[1] Sew solid navy blue 1½×7" inner border strips to top and bottom edges of pillow top center. Join solid navy blue 1½×7" inner border strips to remaining edges (**Diagram 1**). Press seams toward inner border.

DIAGRAM 1

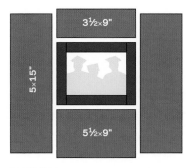

DIAGRAM 2

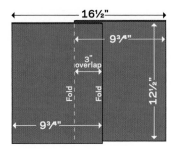

DIAGRAM 3

APPLIQUÉ PLACEMENT DIAGRAM

[2] Sew blue print 3½×9" outer border strip to top edge and blue print 5½×9" outer border strip to bottom edge of pillow top center (**Diagram 2**). Press seams toward outer border. Sew blue print 5×15" outer border strips to remaining edges to make pillow top. Press seams toward outer border. The pillow top should be 18×15" including seam allowances.

appliqué pillow top

[1] Referring to **Appliqué Placement Diagram**, position yellow appliqués on pillow top. Fuse in place.

[2] Layer white flannel 19×16" lining rectangle atop wrong side of pillow top; baste (the flannel adds body and acts as a stabilizer for the appliqués). With matching thread, machine-blanket-stitch around each appliqué.

[3] Trim pillow top to 16½×12½" including seam allowances.

[4] Referring to photo, *opposite*, for placement, machine- or hand-stitch balloon lines onto the pillow top using white thread.

[5] Referring to photo for placement, sew balloon-shape buttons onto pillow top.

finish pillow

[1] With wrong side inside, fold two blue print 12½×19½" rectangles in half to make two 12½×9¾" double-thick pillow back rectangles. Overlap folded edges by 3" to make 16½×12½" pillow back (**Diagram 3**). Baste along all edges to secure pieces.

[2] With right sides together, layer pillow top and pillow back; pin or baste edges. Sew together through all layers. Turn right side out through opening in pillow back and insert pillow form to complete pillow.

tee *time*

Whether from sports teams, school activities, or other events, create a keepsake by turning favorite T-shirts into a memory-filled quilt.

QUILTMAKER **PAULINE RICHARDS**   QUILTER **KAREN GILSON**   PHOTOGRAPHERS **ADAM ALBRIGHT, MARTY BALDWIN AND CRAIG ANDERSON**

materials

- 15 or more T-shirts with logos
- 6 or more solid-color plain T-shirts
- ⅝ yard solid black (binding)
- 4 yards backing fabric
- 70×81" batting
- 10 yards fusible tricot interfacing

Finished quilt: 64×75"

Quantities are for 44/45"-wide, 100% cotton fabrics. Measurements include a ½" seam allowance. Sew with right sides together unless otherwise stated.

prepare t-shirts

Some people think sewing stretchy fabrics is tough, but we've made it easy by giving you the secret—fusible tricot interfacing. Without adding a lot of bulk, this lightweight knit interfacing prevents T-shirt knit from stretching out of shape while you're cutting and sewing. Look for interfacing brand names such as So Sheer or Fusi-Knit.

The greatest stretch of most T-shirts goes around the body (crosswise). To stabilize the shirts, place the interfacing so its stretch goes opposite the T-shirt's stretchiest direction. (Ususally, this means putting the interfacing's greatest stretch running lengthwise.)

[1] Cut each T-shirt up the sides and across the top to separate the front and back; remove the sleeves.

[2] Cut large rectangles of fusible tricot interfacing to cover the fronts and backs of the T-shirts you're using.

[3] Place each T-shirt front or back wrong side up on your work surface. With greatest stretch going in opposite directions, place fusible-web rectangles on T-shirts, fusible side down. Following the manufacturer's instructions, fuse in place; let cool.

tip

Making a T-shirt quilt as a graduation gift? Include a few light-color T-shirts in your quilt where friends and family can add their autographs and well-wishes using a fabric marker.

[4] Divide prepared T-shirts with logos into two piles— a narrow pile (logos that will fit best in a 6"-wide finished row) and a wide pile (logos that will fit better in a 13"-wide finished row). (Depending on the size of T-shirts you're using, you may wish to adapt the width of your rows to better accommodate the logos.)

cut logo rectangles

From each interfaced logo shirt in wide pile, cut:
▸ 1—14"-wide rectangle, centering logo across width and cutting at least 1" above and below logo where possible

From each interfaced logo shirt in narrow pile, cut:
▸ 1—7"-wide rectangle, centering logo across width and cutting at least 1" above and below logo where possible

cut remaining fabrics

The quilt top will be assembled in seven vertical rows—four narrow and three wide (**Quilt Assembly Diagram**). To cut the solid-color rectangles you'll need to fill in the spaces between logo rectangles, refer to the following:

Wide rows: Add heights of 14"-wide logo rectangles (subtracting 1" from each height for seam allowances). Subtract this amount from 250" to get an estimated total amount needed.

Narrow rows: Add heights of 7"-wide logo rectangles (subtracting 1" from each height for seam allowances). Subtract this amount from 350" to get an estimated total amount needed.

QUILT ASSEMBLY DIAGRAM

From interfaced solid-color plain shirts and scraps of remaining logo shirts, cut:

▸ Enough 14"-wide rectangles in heights varying from 2" to 6" to equal amount determined above

▸ Enough 7"-wide rectangles in heights varying from 2" to 20" to equal amount determined above

From solid black, cut:

▸ 8—2½×42" binding strips

assemble quilt top

[1] Referring to **Quilt Assembly Diagram** on *page 140*, lay out all pieces in seven vertical rows, distributing logo rectangles evenly throughout the rows.

[2] Join pieces in each row using a ½" seam allowance to make four narrow rows and three wide rows. Press all seams open. If necessary, trim each row to 75" long.

[3] Join all rows to complete quilt top. Press seams open.

finish quilt

[1] Layer quilt top, batting, and backing; baste. (For details, see Complete the Quilt, *page 158*.)

[2] Quilt as desired. This quilt was stitched with variegated thread in an allover stipple.

[3] Bind with solid black binding strips. (For details, see Better Binding, *page 159*.)

give yourself a break!

A quilt made of all T-shirts can be heavy and awkward to machine-quilt, so consider hiring a long-arm quilting professional to do the job. Ask your local quilt shop to recommend a quilter or find one near you at www.quiltprofessionals.com. Just like the clothes it's made from, your quilt will probably get a lot of wear and tear; have it more densely quilted to help it retain its shape after washing. Choose a polyester or cotton/poly-blend batting to avoid adding extra weight.

color option

If you're not interested in making quilts from T-shirts, try the fat-quarter-friendly variation of "Blanket Statement" above, which uses cotton prints from Moda Fabrics' Quilt Pink collection. To make it even easier, we eliminated the narrow rows.

For the 91½×91" quilt, cut 30 fat quarters into 28—13½×17½" rectangles and 35—13½×5" rectangles. Mix and match rectangles in seven vertical rows of five small rectangles and four large rectangles each, then join with ¼" seams.

One pattern equals three looks to satisfy your favorite teen's ever-changing tastes.

PHOTOGRAPHER **CAMERON SADEGHPOUR**

pillow *perfect*

materials

- ¼ yard print No. 1 (blocks)
- ⅛ yard print No. 2 (blocks)
- ¼ yard print No. 3 (sashing strips)
- ⅛ yard print No. 4 (sashing squares)
- 1 yard print No. 5 (pillowcase body)

Finished pillowcase: 28½×19⅝" (fits a standard-size bed pillow)   Finished block: 3½" square

Quantities are for 44/45"-wide, 100% cotton fabrics. Measurements include ¼" seam allowances. Sew with right sides together unless otherwise stated.

choosing fabrics

This trio of bordered pillowcases shows what a big difference fabric choice can make. Each pillowcase begins with a main print for the body, to which coordinating tone-on-tones and smaller-scale prints are added.

cut fabrics

To make the best use of your fabrics, cut pieces in the following order.

From print No. 1, cut:
- 16—2⅝" squares, cutting each in half diagonally for 32 triangles total

From print No. 2, cut:
- 8—3" squares

From print No. 3, cut:
- 25—1¾×4" sashing strips

From print No. 4, cut:
- 18—1¾" sashing squares

From print No. 5, cut:
- 1—22×39¾" rectangle
- 1—8¾×39¾" rectangle

assemble blocks

Sew print No. 1 triangles to opposite edges of a print No. 2 square (**Diagram 1**). Press seams toward triangles. Add print No. 1 triangles to square's remaining edges to complete Square-in-a-Square block (**Diagram 2**). Press seams toward triangles. The block should be 4" square including seam allowances. Repeat to make eight Square-in-a-Square blocks total.

assemble border

[1] Alternating 1¾×4" print No. 3 sashing strips and blocks, sew together nine sashing strips and eight Square-in-a-Square blocks to make a block row. Press seams toward sashing strips.

[2] Alternating sashing squares and strips, join nine 1¾" print No. 4 sashing squares and eight print No. 3 sashing strips to make a sashing row. Press seams toward sashing strips. Repeat to make a second sashing row.

[3] Referring to **Diagram 3**, join sashing and block rows to make border. Border should be 6½×39¾" including seam allowances.

assemble pillowcase

[1] Sew together border and print No. 5 rectangles to make a pillowcase unit (**Diagram 3**).

[2] With right side inside, fold pillowcase unit in half. Sew along long raw edges and short, unpieced end of pillowcase unit. Turn right side out and press.

[3] Fold raw edge of pillowcase unit under ½" and press. Fold same edge under 7", leaving a 1"-wide strip along outside edge of border

(**Diagram 3**). From pillowcase right side, stitch in the ditch on border's lower edge to complete pillowcase.

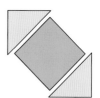

DIAGRAM 1

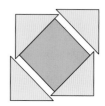

DIAGRAM 2

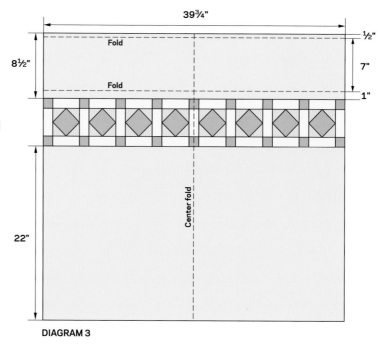

DIAGRAM 3

tip

Whenever you finish a sewing project, gather the remaining fabrics and make one or two pillowcases. Add a solid-color fabric for the body of the pillowcase and use the scraps for the blocks and sashing.

all *squared* up

Bright, lively colors pair up with angular shapes to create a unique throw that's perfect for a dorm room or for simply lounging around.

DESIGNER **PATTY MURPHY**   QUILTER **CAROL JAYNES**   PHOTOGRAPHER **CAMERON SADEGHPOUR**

materials

- 48—10½" squares of assorted batiks or 48—9×22" pieces (fat eighths) of assorted batiks (See Choosing Fabrics for more information.)
- ⅓ yard mottled bright yellow (inner border)
- ⅝ yard mottled royal blue (middle border)
- 1½ yards blue-green leaf batik (outer border)
- ⅔ yard blue-green floral batik (binding)
- 4⅞ yards backing fabric
- 71×87" batting

Finished quilt: 64½×80½"   Finished block: 8" square

Quantities are for 44/45"-wide, 100% cotton fabrics. Measurements include ¼" seam allowances. Sew with right sides together unless otherwise stated.

choosing fabrics

Designer Patty Murphy planned the featured quilt to utilize 10½" squares. If you follow the cutting method detailed in these instructions, you'll have very little fabric waste. If you're concerned about cutting errors, consider buying a few extra squares.

If you don't wish to use 10½" squares, substitute 9×22" pieces (fat eighths) of 48 different batiks.

cut fabrics for blocks

If you're using 10½" squares, refer to **Cutting Diagram** to cut necessary pieces from each assorted batik square.

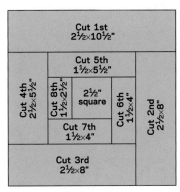

CUTTING DIAGRAM

(Patty recommends cutting six squares at a time to speed the cutting process.) Cut the longest piece along the top edge, then continue cutting clockwise around square. (Pieces will be the correct width, but will need to be trimmed to the length specified in cutting instructions before or during assembly of Log Cabin blocks.)

If you're using fat eighths, cut pieces the exact sizes listed below; first cut two 2½"-wide strips and one 1½"-wide strips the length of the fabric, then subcut into specified lengths.

From each assorted batik, cut:
- 1—2½×8½" strip
- 2—2½×6½" strips
- 1—2½×4½" strip
- 1—1½×4½" strip
- 2—1½×3½" strips
- 1—1½×2½" strip
- 1—2½" square

cut remaining fabrics

From mottled bright yellow, cut:
- 6—1½×42" strips for inner border

From mottled royal blue, cut:
- 7—2½×42" strips for middle border

From blue-green leaf batik, cut:
- 8—5½×42" strips for outer border

From blue-green floral batik, cut:
- 8—2½×42" binding strips

assemble blocks

[1] Referring to **Diagram 1**, lay out the following pieces: a 2½" square from one batik; matching pieces from a second batik (a 1½×2½" strip, two 1½×3½" strips, and a 1½×4½" strip); and matching pieces from a third batik (a 2½×4½" strip, two 2½×6½" strips, and a 2½×8½" strip).

[2] Sew the batik No. 2—1½×2½" strip to left edge of the batik 2½" square to make a block center. Press seam toward batik No. 2 strip.

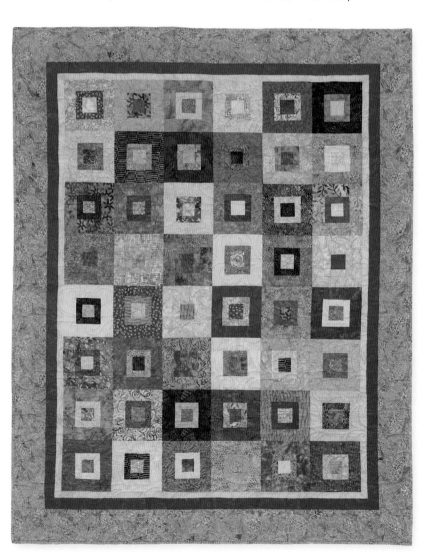

[3] Add a batik No. 2—1½×3½"
strip to bottom edge of
block center; press seam
toward strip just added.
Referring to **Diagram 2**,
continue adding strips to
block center, working
counterclockwise and
pressing each seam toward
the strip just added, to make
a Log Cabin block. The
block should be 8½" square
including seam allowances.

[4] Repeat steps 1 through 3
to make 48 Log Cabin
blocks total. (You will use a
combination of three batiks
for each block, and each
block will have a different
batik No. 1, batik No. 2, and
batik No. 3.) If your blocks
aren't all the same size,
Patty recommends finding
the smallest size and
trimming the larger blocks
to this measurement.
Remember to adjust your
borders to fit when joining
them to the quilt center.

assemble
quilt center

[1] Sew together blocks in
eight horizontal rows (**Quilt
Assembly Diagram**). Press
seams in one direction,
alternating direction with
each row.

[2] Join rows to make quilt
center. Press seams in one
direction. The quilt center
should be 48½×64½"
including seam allowances.

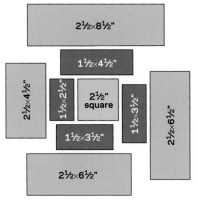

DIAGRAM 1

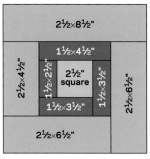

DIAGRAM 2

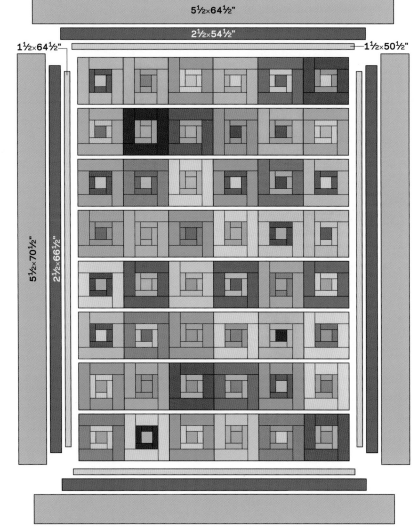

QUILT ASSEMBLY DIAGRAM

assemble and add borders

[1] Cut and piece mottled bright yellow 1½×42" strips to make:
- ▸ 2—1½×64½" inner border strips
- ▸ 2—1½×50½" inner border strips

[2] Sew long inner border strips to long edges of quilt center. Add short inner border strips to remaining edges. Press all seams toward inner border.

[3] Cut and piece mottled royal blue 2½×42" strips to make:
- ▸ 2—2½×66½" middle border strips
- ▸ 2—2½×54½" middle border strips

[4] Sew long middle border strips to long edges of quilt center. Join short middle border strips to remaining edges. Press all seams toward middle border.

[5] Cut and piece blue-green leaf batik 5½×42" strips to make:
- ▸ 2—5½×70½" outer border strips
- ▸ 2—5½×64½" outer border strips

[6] Sew long outer border strips to long edges of quilt center. Join short outer border strips to remaining edges to complete quilt top. Press all seams toward outer border.

finish quilt

[1] Layer quilt top, batting, and backing; baste. (For details, see Complete the Quilt, *page 158*.)

[2] Quilt as desired. This quilt features stitching in an allover large swirl design.

[3] Bind with blue-green floral batik binding strips. (For details, see Better Binding, *page 159*.)

color option

Make "All Squared Up" in flannel and pastels, and you have an irresistibly soft version that makes a great baby gift. Using just 12 blocks, it's framed by three borders in pleasing proportions; finished widths of the inner, middle, and outer borders are 1", 2", and 4" respectively.

quilting
basics

Refer to these tips and techniques
whenever you need information
for your projects.

make and use templates

To make templates, use easy-to-cut transparent template plastic, available at crafts supply stores.

To make a template, lay the plastic over a printed pattern. Trace the pattern using a permanent marker (and ruler for straight lines). Mark template with quilt name, letter, and any marked matching points (**Photo 1**).

For appliqué and hand piecing, the solid lines indicate finished size, and you will add any needed seams as instructed in project.

For machine piecing, the solid lines are cutting lines, and dashed lines are seam lines. (An arrow on a pattern indicates the direction the fabric grain should run.)

Cut out the template and check it against the original pattern for accuracy (**Photo 2**). If it isn't accurate, the error (even if small) will multiply as you assemble a quilt.

Using a pushpin, make a hole in the template at all marked matching points (**Photo 3**). The hole must be large enough to accommodate a pencil point.

To trace the template on fabric, use a pencil, white dressmaker's pencil, chalk,

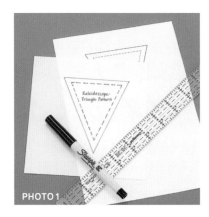

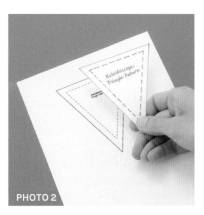

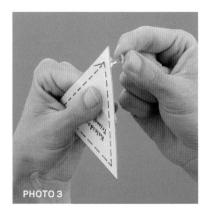

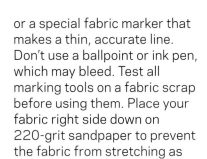

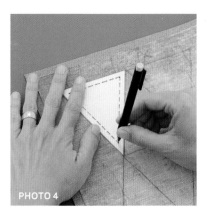

or a special fabric marker that makes a thin, accurate line. Don't use a ballpoint or ink pen, which may bleed. Test all marking tools on a fabric scrap before using them. Place your fabric right side down on 220-grit sandpaper to prevent the fabric from stretching as

you trace. Place the template facedown on the wrong side of the fabric with the template's grain line parallel to the fabric's lengthwise or crosswise grain. Trace around the template. Mark any matching points through the holes in the template (**Photo 4**).

(When sewing pieces together, line up and pin through matching points to ensure accurate assembly.)

Repeat to trace the number of pieces needed, positioning the tracings without space between them. Use scissors or a rotary cutter and ruler to precisely cut fabric pieces on the drawn lines (**Photo 5**).

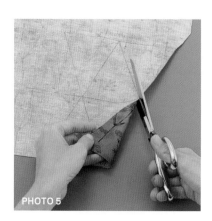

PHOTO 5

piece and appliqué

stitching: Quilting depends upon accuracy at every step. Use exact ¼" seam allowances throughout a quilt's construction. It isn't necessary to backstitch at the beginning of any seam that will be intersected by another seam later in the quiltmaking process. Use a stitch length of 10 to 12 stitches per inch (2.0- to 2.5-mm setting) to prevent stitches from unraveling before they're stitched over again. Secure seams that won't be sewn across again (such as those in borders) with a few backstitches.

pinning: When you want seam lines to line up perfectly, first match up seams of pieced units. Place an extra-fine pin diagonally through the pieces, catching both seam allowances. Avoid sewing over pins, as this can cause damage to your machine and injury to you.

pressing: Pressing seams ensures accurate piecing. Set the seam first by pressing it as it was sewn, without opening up the fabric pieces. This helps sink the stitches into the fabric, leaving you with a less bulky seam allowance.

The direction you press is important and is usually specified in the instructions. Usually, you will press the entire seam to one side rather than open. When two seams will be joined, first press the seams in opposite directions; this helps line up the seams perfectly and reduces bulk.

Press seam allowances in each row in opposite directions so they abut when rows are joined.

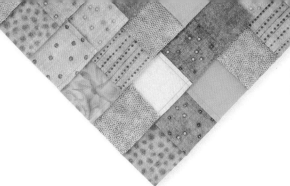

Precise ¼" seams allow you to join units, blocks, and rows with ease.

Make sure you are pressing, not ironing. Ironing means moving the iron while it is in contact with the fabric; this stretches and distorts seams. Pressing is lifting the iron off the surface of the fabric and putting it back down in another location.

machine appliqué: Many fast-and-easy appliqué projects are meant to be fused, then secured with stitching. Follow the directions in the project instructions for how to prepare appliqué pieces for fusing.

Pivoting outside curves. When appliquéing, position the presser foot so the left swing of the needle is on the appliqué and the right swing of the needle is just on the outer edge of the appliqué, grazing the foundation (**Photo 6**).

Stop at the first pivot point with the needle down in the fabric on the right-hand swing of the needle (see first red dot in **Diagram 1**; the arrow indicates the stitching direction). Raise the presser foot, pivot the fabric slightly, and begin stitching to the next pivot point. Repeat as needed to round the entire outer curve.

To help you know when to pivot, mark the edges of circular or oval appliqué pieces with the hours of a clock; pivot the fabric at each mark (**Photo 7**).

Turning outside corners. When turning a corner, knowing where and when to stop and pivot makes a big difference in the finished look of your appliqué stitches.

Stop with the needle down in the fabric on the right-hand swing of the needle (see red dot in **Diagram 2**). Raise the presser foot and pivot the fabric. Lower the presser foot and begin stitching to the next edge (**Diagram 3**).

PHOTO 6

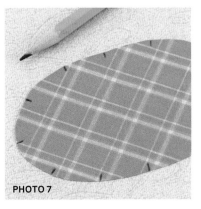

PHOTO 7

tip

If you're having difficulty aligning seams when sewing rows together, try sewing with the seam allowance on top facing away from you as you guide the rows under the presser foot. This forces the top seam to butt up to the lower seam so the two automatically lock together.

DIAGRAM 1

DIAGRAM 2

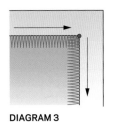

DIAGRAM 3

hand appliqué: To make a project portable, substitute hand appliqué for fusible appliqué. Use a sharp, between, straw, or milliners needle and the finest thread you can find that matches the appliqué pieces. Follow the directions in the project instructions for how to use freezer paper for cutting appliqué shapes.

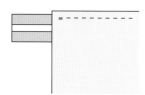

DIAGRAM 4

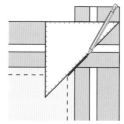

DIAGRAM 5

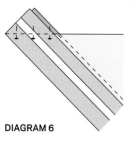

DIAGRAM 6

Slip-stitch the edges. Pin or baste the appliqué to the appliqué foundation. Thread a handsewing needle with 18" of thread. Slip-stitch the appliqué edge in place by passing the needle through the folded edge of the appliqué and then through the appliqué foundation (**Photo 8**). Continue around the appliqué, taking smaller stitches around inside corners and curves.

Finish it up. End the thread by knotting it on the wrong side of the foundation, beneath the appliqué piece. Once all pieces have been appliquéd, place the foundation facedown on a terry cloth towel and press from the wrong side to prevent flattening the appliqués.

mitering borders

To add a border with mitered corners, first pin a border strip to a quilt top edge, matching the center of the strip and the center of the quilt top edge. Sew together, beginning and ending the seam ¼" from the quilt top corners (**Diagram 4**). Allow excess border fabric to extend beyond the edges. Repeat with the remaining border strips. Press the seam allowances toward the border strips.

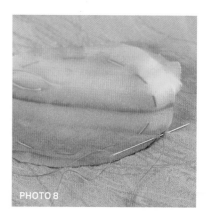

PHOTO 8

At one corner, lap one border strip over the other (**Diagram 5**). Align the edge of a 90° right triangle with the raw edge of the top strip so the long edge of the triangle intersects the border seam in the corner. With a pencil, draw along the edge of the triangle from the seam out to the raw edge. Place the bottom border strip on top and repeat the marking process.

With right sides together, match the marked seam lines and pin (**Diagram 6**).

Beginning with a backstitch at the inside corner, sew together the strips, stitching exactly on the marked lines. Check the right side to see that the corner lies flat. Trim the excess fabric, leaving a ¼" seam allowance. Press the seam open. Mark and sew the remaining corners in the same manner.

PHOTO 9

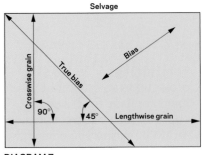

Selvage

Crosswise grain

True bias

Bias

90°

45°

Lengthwise grain

DIAGRAM 7

cutting bias strips

Begin with a fabric square or rectangle. Using an acrylic ruler and rotary cutter, cut one edge at a 45° angle. Measure the desired width from the cut edge, then make a cut parallel to the edge (**Photo 9**). Repeat until you have the desired number of strips. Handle bias strips carefully to avoid distorting the fabric.

cutting on the bias

Bias runs diagonally between the lengthwise or crosswise grain line of a woven fabric. The "true" bias runs exactly at a 45° angle to the grain lines (**Diagram 7**) and has the most stretch in a woven fabric.

Because of their built-in stretch, strips cut on the bias can be easily curved or shaped. Use them when binding curved edges or to make curved appliqué pieces like vines or stems.

You can also cut directional fabrics like plaids or stripes on the bias for purely visual reasons. A bias binding cut from a stripe fabric creates a barber pole effect.

complete the quilt

choose your batting: Batting comes in different fibers (cotton, polyester, wool, and silk), and its loft can range greatly—from 1/8" to 1" or more. Generally, choose a low to medium loft for hand or machine quilting and a high loft for tied quilts. Pay attention to the manufacturer's label, which recommends the maximum distance between rows of quilting. If you exceed this distance, the batting will shift and bunch later, resulting in a lumpy quilt.

tip

Keep needles for hand stitching in good condition by wiping the surface after use and storing them in the original packaging.

Double-layer binding is easy to apply and adds durability to your finished quilt.

assemble the layers: Cut and piece the backing fabric to measure at least 3" bigger on all sides than the quilt top. Press seams open. Place the quilt backing wrong side up on a large, flat surface. Center and smooth the batting in place atop the quilt backing. Center the quilt top right side up on top of the batting and smooth out any wrinkles. Use safety pins or long hand stitches to baste all the layers together.

trim quilt: Trim the batting and backing fabric even with the quilt top edges; machine-baste a scant ¼" from quilt top edges if desired. (Some quilters prefer to wait until they have machine-sewn the binding to the quilt top before trimming the batting and backing.)

quilt as desired: A few of the more common machine-quilting methods follow.

Stitching in the ditch. Stitch just inside a seam line; the stitches should almost disappear into the seam. Using a walking foot attachment on your sewing machine will help prevent the quilt layers from shifting.

Stipple quilting. This random, allover stitching provides texture and interest behind a pattern. Use a darning foot and lower the feed dogs on your machine.

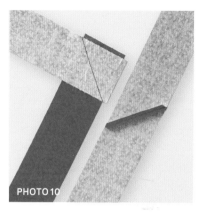
PHOTO 10

Place binding strips perpendicular to each other and stitch. Trim and press seams open to reduce bulk.

Outline quilting. Stitch ¼" from a seam line or the edge of an appliqué shape, just past the extra thickness of the seam allowance.

better binding

cut the strips: The cutting instructions for each project tell you the width and how many binding strips to cut. Unless otherwise specified, cut binding strips on the straight grain of the fabric. Join the binding strips with diagonal seams (**Photo 10**) to make one long binding strip. Trim seams to ¼" and press open.

To baste layers together, work from the center of the quilt out. Pin or stitch, spacing the pins or stitches 3" to 4" apart.

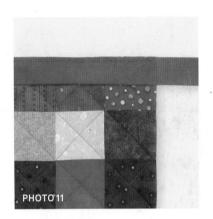

PHOTO 11

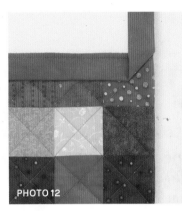

PHOTO 12

PHOTO 13

attach the binding: With the wrong side inside, fold under 1" at one end of the binding strip and press. Then fold the strip in half lengthwise with the wrong side inside. Place the binding strip against the right side of the quilt top along one edge, aligning the binding strip's raw edges with the quilt top's raw edge (do not start at a corner). Begin sewing the binding in place 2" from the folded end.

turn the corner: Stop sewing when you're ¼" from the corner (or a distance equal to the seam allowance you're using). Backstitch, then clip the threads (**Photo 11**). Remove the quilt from under the sewing-machine presser foot. Fold the binding strip upward, creating a diagonal fold, and finger-press (**Photo 12**). Holding the diagonal fold in place with your finger, bring the binding strip down in line with the next edge, making a horizontal fold that aligns with the quilt edge. Start sewing again at the top of the horizontal fold, stitching through all layers (**Photo 13**). Sew around the quilt, turning each corner in the same manner.

finish it up: When you return to the starting point, encase the binding strip's raw edge inside the folded end and finish sewing to the starting point. Trim the batting and backing fabric even with the quilt top edges if not done earlier.

Turn the binding over the edge to the back. Hand-stitch the binding to the backing fabric only, covering any machine stitching. To make the binding corners on the quilt back match the mitered corners on the quilt front, hand-stitch up to a corner and make a fold in the binding. Secure the fold with a couple stitches, then continue stitching the binding in place along the next edge.

tip

If your quilting is more than 1" from the outer edges, baste the layers together around the quilt ⅜" from the edges. This will prevent the outside edges from ruffling and stretching as the binding is applied.